THE WEST GERMANS

HOW THEY LIVE AND WORK

Volumes in the series:

THE FRENCH, by Joseph T. Carroll
THE ITALIANS, by Andrew Bryant
THE SPANIARDS, by Michael Perceval
THE WEST GERMANS, by Reginald Peck

The West Germans
HOW THEY LIVE AND WORK

Reginald Peck

PRAEGER PUBLISHERS
New York . Washington

Southwest College
CITY COLLEGES OF CHICAGO
7500 SOUTH PULASKI ROAD
CHICAGO, ILLINOIS   60652

BOOKS THAT MATTER

Published in the United States of America in 1970
by Praeger Publishers, Inc.
111 Fourth Avenue, New York, N.Y. 10003

© 1969 in London, England, by Reginald Peck

All rights reserved

Library of Congress Catalog Card Number: 74-93740

Printed in Great Britain

Contents

	INTRODUCTION	11
I	THE COUNTRY AND THE PEOPLE	14

Chief physical characteristics . racial origins . population . language . national characteristics . religion . historical landmarks

II	HOW THE COUNTRY IS RUN	40

Federal government . political parties . local government . the ministries . the currency . taxation . police . justice . the Nazi legacy . Nazi criminals . lawyers . the armed forces

III	THE REGIONS	67

Bavaria . Lower Saxony . Baden-Württemberg . North Rhine-Westphalia . Schleswig-Holstein . Hesse . Hamburg . Bremen . Rhineland-Palatinate . The Saarland . Berlin

IV	HOW THEY LIVE	94

Housing . heating and household equipment . servants . food and drink . how they spend their money . social security . health services

V	HOW THEY WORK	113

Industry . coal . oil . gas . electricity . atom power . other mineral resources . iron and steel . motor vehicles . electro-technical . chemicals . engineering and machinery . shipbuilding . aircraft . handicraft . agriculture . fisheries . forestry . trade . trade unions and employers' associations . employment and unemployment . trade fairs and exhibitions . foreign trade . finance

VI	HOW THEY LEARN	145
VII	HOW THEY GET ABOUT	152
	Railways . roads . waterways . air traffic	
VIII	HOW THEY AMUSE THEMSELVES	158
	Theatre and music . films . radio and television . books . museums and art galleries . the press . sport . holidays	
IX	HINTS FOR VISITORS	174
	INDEX	181

List of Illustrations

	Page
The east-west German border near Grafhorst	17
The Brandenburg Gate	17
Wedding in Cologne (*Courtesy: Tourist Office, Cologne*)	18
Zither players in Kochel, Bavaria (*Courtesy: Central office for Tourism, Frankfurt a/M*)	18
The Schildergasse in Cologne (*Courtesy: Central Office for Tourism, Frankfurt a/M*)	35
Modern German housing near Bad Godesberg	35
Nuclear research in Jülich	36
At work on a ship's turbine	36
A potter at work	53
A glass school in Cologne	53
Oil and Chemical works between Bonn and Cologne	54
Steelworks in Dortmund	54
Production of Volkswagen cars at the main works at Wolfsburg (*Courtesy: The Volkswagen Works, Wolfsburg*)	71
Liquid Gas containers at Hamburg	71
Tractors are rapidly replacing oxen and horses on German farms	72
Gathering grapes for wine in the Palatinate	72
At school in Bad Godesberg	89
Munich University	89

Traffic control by television	90
New roads and a new bridge in Cologne	90
Autobahn across the Hasel valley in the Spessart (*Courtesy: Central Office of Tourism, Frankfurt a/M*)	107
Crossing the Rhine by overhead gondola at Cologne (*Courtesy: Tourist Office, Cologne*)	107
Old wine house at Bacharach on the Rhine	108
Dinkelsbühl in Bavaria (*Courtesy: Central Office for Tourism, Frankfurt a/M*)	108
Gymnastics in West Berlin	125
The international film festival in West Berlin	125
Carnival time in Baden-Württemberg (*Courtesy: Central Office for Tourism, Frankfurt a/M*)	126
Carnival time in the Rhineland	126
At the top of the Zugspitze in Bavaria	143
Carnival time in Bavaria	143
The August Thyssen headquarters in Düsseldorf (*Courtesy: Central Office for Tourism, Frankfurt a/M*)	144
Rothenburg ob der Tauber	144

Plates not otherwise acknowledged are by kind permission of The Federal Press and Information Office, Bonn

Map
General map of Germany

The author is indebted to so many officials at federal, state and municipal level for the statistical and factual information they have provided that it would be difficult to list them all. But he believes they will not take it amiss if he names Frau Braune of the Federal Press and Information Office in Bonn, who, by almost snatching from the printing presses the latest facts and figures as they appeared, enabled the book to be more up to date than it could otherwise have been.

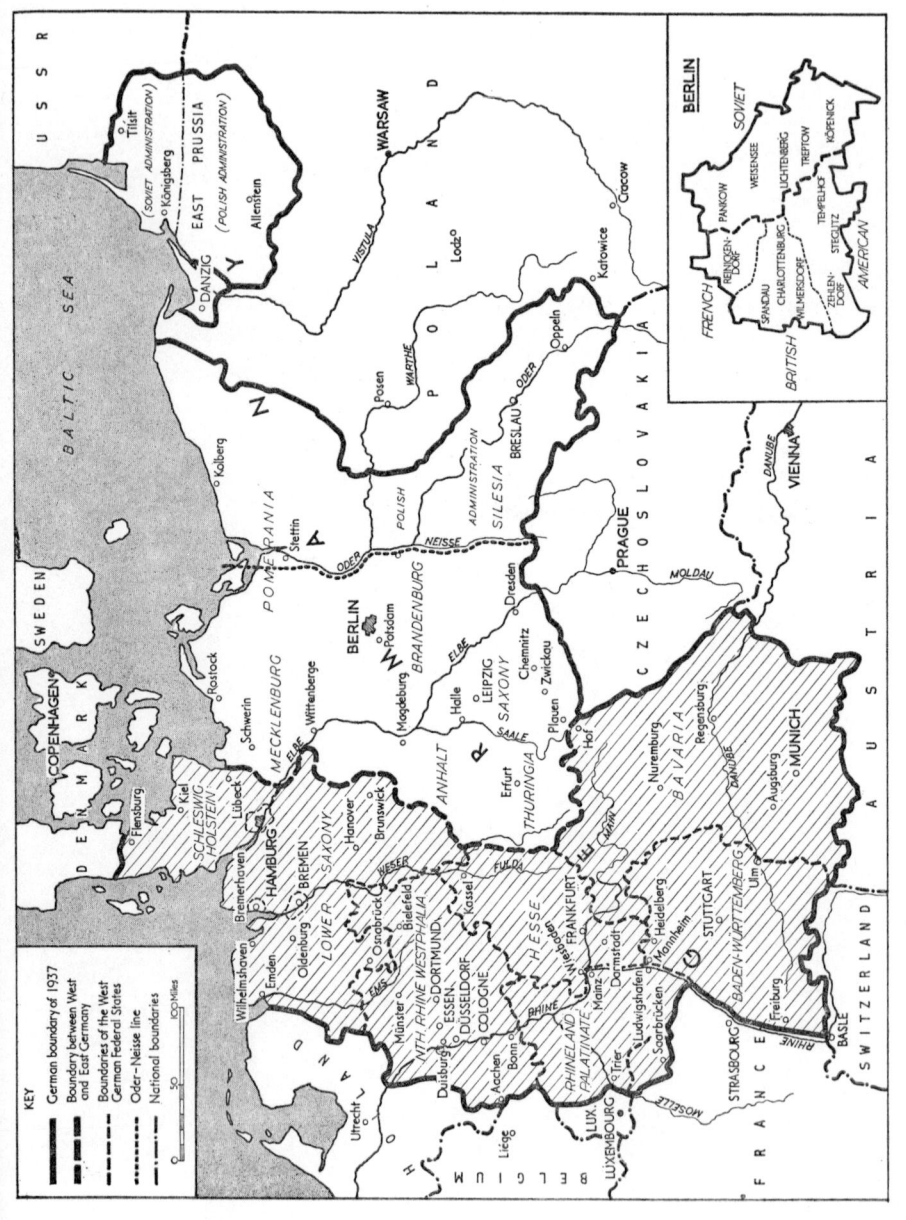

Introduction

THE territories with which this book is concerned are referred to in the pages that follow as 'West Germany,' and it is as such that they are known generally in the outside world. But their official title is The Federal Republic of Germany (*Die Bundesrepublik Deutschland*), and that is the name (or the shorter form *Die Bundesrepublik*) used in both speech and writing by the people who inhabit them. The 'East Germany' of familiar usage bears the official title The German Democratic Republic (*Die Deutsche Demokratische Republik*) in Communist countries but not elsewhere.

Behind this apparently unimportant difference of nomenclature—in which the outside world generally is concerned only to use the form it finds most convenient to the tongue—lurks one of the most intractable political problems of our time. It is the whole question of the reunification of the Germany that was dismembered once after the First World War and again—though differently—after the second.

The people who live in the Federal Republic avoid the name 'West Germany,' not only because it is not strictly correct but also because it would seem to justify by implication the use by the outside world of 'East Germany' for the German Democratic Republic. To them 'East Germany' means those territories that before the First World War were part of Germany but which are now held by Poland and in part also by Russia (see Chapter I).

But the complications are not yet at an end. If the West Germans dislike the name 'East Germany' for the territories to which it is commonly applied, they dislike the name 'German Democratic Republic' even more. They do not officially recognise the existence of any such state or country or political unit of any kind.

This has involved the West Germans in a dilemma of growing complexity. The most conservative of them still use the old expression 'Russian Zone of Occupation,' although the western equivalents—British, American, French Zones of Occupation—were dropped many years ago. An acceptable though little used alternative is 'Middle Germany.' But as cold war attitudes slowly pass, the need has been felt for a more realistic term. The earlier phrase, 'so-called' Democratic Republic, began to seem silly as well as cumbersome, and because of the resentment it caused to the Communist authorities of 'East Germany' it stood in the way of the détente between the two sides towards which some politicians in the west were beginning to grope. So such curious phrases as 'the other side' came into somewhat coy use in the west—with the hope in the minds of those who devised them that they would give offence neither to the die-hard conservatives in the west nor the Communist authorities in the east. Some very bold spirits in the west occasionally went so far as to refer to the German Democratic Republic without the hitherto obligatory 'so-called.' The outcry was such that it is heard now only on the rarest occasions.

The terms 'West Germany' and even 'West Germans' thus beg many questions—among them whether the adjective should be spelled with a capital on the ground that it gives a political significance to what should be only a geographical distinction. But they are the terms known to and used by the potential readers of this book—and are, in their minds, for the most part neutral. The adjective has been omitted in a few places, partly for the sake of avoiding constant repetition, though occasionally because it would have been inaccurate where reference is made to a larger 'Germany.' In no case does the terminology used imply the taking of sides by the author on what is—aside from the responsibilities of the four former occupying powers for reunification—an internal German matter.

These hair-splitting differences may seem tiresome and confusing to the outside world and not worth the trouble of understanding. But they are none the less the very stuff of European and indeed world politics. There can be no final east-west settlement until the problems they conceal are resolved.

Note on exchange rates. The rates of exchange used in converting statistics in this book from the mark into sterling and dollars are mainly the ones in force during the period from which most of them derive—i.e. after the West German revaluation of March 1961 but before the British devaluation of November 1967. The rates are £1=DM 11.20 and $1=DM 4. Exceptions are the chapters on How they Amuse Themselves and Hints to Visitors, where a few current prices are converted at current rates, i.e. £1=DM 9.60. The dollar remained unaffected at $1=DM 4.

I

The Country and the People

CHIEF PHYSICAL CHARACTERISTICS

WEST GERMANY comprises rather less than half the larger Germany that was dismembered by the victors at the end of the Second World War. Substantial territories in the east are now held by Poland, and smaller ones by Russia, while the rest is divided between what became, after a period of military occupation, separate east and west German states. Whether these changes can be regarded as permanent will be considered later in this chapter. The larger Germany within the boundaries of 1937 comprised about one-tenth of the whole of Europe (excluding European Russia), and was, after France and Spain, the largest country in Europe. It lay between 47 and 55 N and 6 and 23 E. In the north, Moscow and Labrador are on the same parallel, and in the south, Rostov and Seattle. The West Germany with which this book is concerned has an area of 95,959 square miles, which makes it comparable in size with Britain and with the American state of Oregon. The maximum distance from north to south is 517 miles and from east to west 281 miles. Its central position in Europe gives it many neighbours —Denmark, Holland, Belgium, France and Luxemburg in the north and west, Austria and Switzerland in the south, and Czechoslovakia in the east. By one of many post-war anomalies West Berlin lies some 100 miles inside East Germany and is thus cut off from the main body of the country.

The flat lands of the northern part of West Germany belong to the great north German plain, which is an eastward extension of the Flemish lowlands and which continues on to the east

The Country and the People

European plain. The maximum height is only 984 feet, and the area is characterised by sandy soil and stretches of heath and moorland. The plain is bounded in the north by the North Sea and the Baltic, which give the country its only clearly defined, natural frontiers. In the Baltic are Fehmarn and other islands, and in the North Sea the small group of Frisian islands and (farther out to sea) Heligoland.

South of the flat lands a central escarpment of hill-country rises in the Harz to a height of 3,747 feet (the Brocken peak, which is, however, in East Germany). It includes also much fertile land and the slate hills of the Eifel and the Hunsrück. The scenery of this area is varied and attractive.

Still further south are lowlands surrounded by the high Black Forest, the Odenwald and the Haardt. This area also includes the Swabian-Franconian terrace land and the Bavarian forest. The highest point is the Feldberg (4,905 feet) in the Black Forest.

Finally, in the south, foothills rise to the Bavarian alps where, in the rugged Wetterstein range, the Zugspitze (9,700 feet) is the highest peak in the entire country. Lake Constance, in the south, is bordered by Austria and Switzerland as well as by West Germany. Its total area is 208 square miles but, since the frontier runs through it, the area inside West Germany is only 118 square miles.

The Rhine flows out of Lake Constance to form the boundary, first between West Germany and Switzerland, and then between West Germany and France. It is then inside West Germany until it crosses Holland to enter the North Sea at Rotterdam. Its length, below Lake Constance, is 537 miles, and it remains today, as it has been throughout the centuries, a vital communications link between southern Europe and the north. The Danube rises in southern Germany and flows for 402 miles to Passau, where it enters Austria. The Elbe (435 miles), coming from Czechoslovakia, crosses first East and then West Germany and flows into the North Sea north-west of the great port of Hamburg, which stands on its banks.

The German climate is temperate but very changeable. Prevailing winds are westerly, and rain is liable to fall at any period of the year. The amount varies from 20 to 28 inches in the northern flat lands, from 27 to 40 inches in the central escarpment, and up to 80 inches in the Alps of the south. Temperatures are nowhere extreme—from 34F to 27F in January (the coldest month) at sea level, and to 21F in the mountains. In summer (mid-July) temperatures in the north rise to 61F, and in sheltered mountain valleys to 68F. The annual average is 48F. The highest mountains, whether in the Harz, the Black Forest or the Alps, are generally snow-covered from January to March.

Germany has abundant supplies of coal, including brown coal (lignite), considerable deposits of potash salts, though these are now largely in East Germany, some oil, a little iron, and supplies as yet not fully determined of natural gas. The use made of these resources is examined in the chapter on How they Work.

Some 29 per cent of the total area of West Germany is covered by woodland. Conifers predominate, but there are large quantities of beech, birch, lime trees and oaks.

The east-west German border near Grafhorst.

The Brandenburg Gate at the boundary between east and west Berlin. It is partly concealed by the dividing wall built by the Communists in August 1961.

RACIAL ORIGINS

The blond, blue-eyed 'Nordic' race of Hitler's disordered imagination did not exist in his own day and age, and had not done so for many centuries. But we have the authority of Tacitus for saying that the 'Germanen' of whom he wrote in the first century A.D. were 'blue-eyed and defiant in their gaze' and they had 'reddish-blond hair.' Their bodies were 'finely developed,' but they exerted themselves 'only when attacking the enemy.' They showed 'no love of daily work and could not endure thirst or heat.' On the other hand they endured hunger, and the raw climate in which they lived, with great fortitude.

But, since Tacitus, the blood of the tribesmen of whom he wrote has been mingling for centuries with that of Slav and other neighbours from all quarters of the compass, so that the Germans of today are as mixed and mongrel as any other people.

Tacitus was uncertain as to where the 'Germanen' came from, but in a commonsense way he concluded, from the evidence at his disposal, that they were probably the original inhabitants of

---

Wedding in the foreground—Cologne cathedral in the background.

Zither players in Kochel, Bavaria.

the lands in which he found them. No one would have been so foolish, he wrote, as to brave the journey from the quiet waters of the Mediterranean to the rough seas of the north in order to live in such an uninviting country as 'Germania.' Still less could he imagine that any race in its senses would willingly exchange 'the blooming provinces of Asia Minor or North Africa or Italy' for such a place and such a climate. The only possible conclusion was that the 'Germanen' had lived in 'Germania' from the start—whenever that might have been. Later authorities have recorded that the Germanic tribes emerged from the Teutonic branch (see this chapter, Language) of the Indo-Germanic language family. Some of them—the Saxons—played an important part in the formation of early England, while others—the Franks—did the same for France. Other *stämme*—tribes— were the Frisians in the north, the Thuringians in the central part of the country, the *Alemanni* (from whom the French derive their name for Germans—*Allemands*) and the Bavarians in the south.

The broad conclusion is that one German might be mistaken for a Briton, another might pass as a Pole, another as an Italian, yet another as a Frenchman or a Dutchman and so on. There is no standard 'German' any more than there is a standard Briton, American, etc.

POPULATION

The population of West Germany is (1969) about 60 million. This is about 5 million more than Britain and thirty times as many as the American state of Oregon, both of which have an area similar to that of West Germany. The density of population, at 624 per square mile, compares with 578 in Britain and 54 in the United States, where the total population of some 200 million is distributed over a vastly greater area than either Britain or West Germany. Immediately before the Second World War 43 million people lived in the area now known as West Germany. But the increase has not all been natural. Nearly

12 million people fled from the East German territories as the Russian armies advanced, or were driven out when Poland and Russia took control of those areas. Some of these expellees, as they are called, settled in the area now known as East Germany, but most—about 8 million—came on to West Germany. Following this early, forced migration came what was at first a steady drift, and later a powerful flow, of persons from East to West Germany. They were not physically ejected like the earlier millions from still further east, but they fled voluntarily as the Communist grip on East Germany tightened. Many of them—political and trade union leaders and others—were in genuine danger of life or liberty, but the majority came because they found the way of life imposed by the Russian-backed Communist authorities intolerable. At times the numbers coming west—mostly via Berlin where the crossing was, in the early years, unrestricted—reached several thousands a day, and had reached some 3 million by the time the Communists became alarmed at the loss of population and erected their notorious wall. Since then—August 1961—movement from east to west, whether via Berlin or the 850-mile zonal border, has increasingly involved the risk of life and limb. Guards on the ground or in watch-towers are heavily armed and equipped with tracker dogs and searchlights, and 'death strips' are ploughed to reveal footprints and studded with land mines. Audacious attempts to get through or over or under these various lethal obstacles were, in the first year or two, occasionally successful, but their numbers have dropped to the point where those who get over safely are no more than a hundred or two a year. Many have been shot in the attempt or maimed by land mines. The erection of the wall was a breach of the four-power agreements on Berlin; it produced a world crisis, but was almost completely successful in its purpose.

Meantime, although the increase in the number of births has wiped out wartime losses in a purely numerical sense, there is still a shortage of able-bodied males. By 1961 the average size of a family, which in 1871 had been 4.6 persons, had decreased to 2.7. By the same year the number of one-person households had risen from 8.4 per cent (1933) to 20.6 per cent. Around 1860 some 70 per cent of all married couples had three or more children, but for the last century the two-child family has predominated. By June 1960 hardly more than 19 per cent of all families had more than two children and, according to the latest statistics, one marriage in six will in the near future be entirely childless.

In the world's birth statistics, the birth rate in West Germany (together with Austria) is about the lowest—at 17.7 per thousand inhabitants (1965) compared with 40.6 in 1875. But since infant mortality has greatly decreased, the rate of increase of the population has not been correspondingly affected. In 1965 it was down to 23.8 per thousand live births, of which the number was 1,044,000. The average age at which men got married was 28.5, and women married on the average at 25.3. The age structure of the population has greatly changed as a result of the increase in the expectation of life over the last ninety years: from 37 to 70 years.

During the period from 1954 to 1965 inclusive, foreigners and stateless persons coming into West Germany included 86,000 from the United States, 45,000 from Canada and 24,000 from Australia. During the same period 292,000 persons left the country for the United States, 66,000 for Australia and 19,000 for South Africa. Excluding foreign workers, whose numbers reached a maximum in 1965 of 1,200,000 (and fell to below 1 million in 1966-7 and began rising again in 1968), there are about one per cent of foreigners in West Germany. There is a very small Danish minority in Schleswig-Holstein.

There are 24,000 independent political communities in West Germany, of which 57 are large towns inhabited by some 20 million people. Of these major centres of population, 25 are in the great industrial state of North Rhine-Westphalia, which includes the Ruhr. The cities (over one million inhabitants) are three in number—West Berlin (2.2 million inhabitants), Hamburg (1.9 million) and Munich (1.2 million). Bonn, the federal capital, has a population of 143,000. The smallest community in the country is Hauenstein, with a population of 175.

The Country and the People

There is a general world trend just now away from large towns, and six of them in West Germany have lost three per cent of their population over the past few years. Only three showed an increase of more than ten per cent. The partial reversal of the earlier and much lamented 'drift to the towns' is a result of improved communications, especially the growth in motorisation, which enables large numbers of people to indulge their preference for life, if not right in the country, at least beyond the confines of the towns in which they work. Of the total population of West Germany, some 21 per cent live in villages of fewer than 2,000 inhabitants, 45 per cent in small and medium-sized towns, and the rest in large towns or cities.

LANGUAGE

The only official language of the country is German, and it is spoken by everyone except the fluctuating foreign population of something like a million. It is a branch of the Indo-Germanic or Indo-European group that in various forms today covers Scandinavia, Holland, and parts of Belgium, as well as Germany itself, Austria and parts of Switzerland. In the three last-named countries the form used in speech and writing (not including the Swiss-dialect German which is spoken only by the Swiss among themselves) is, with relatively minor variations, known as High German (*Hochdeutsch*). In Scandinavia the separate, though among themselves closely similar, Swedish, Norwegian and Danish languages developed. In Holland and parts of Belgium the language of today derives from *Niederdeutsch* (Lower German). English, as spoken today, has the same basic foundations as the others in the group, but as a result of the Roman and still more of the Norman conquest was powerfully influenced by Latin. Early English derived from the language used by the Angles and Saxons (Germanic tribes), and was called Anglo-Saxon. The early language from which High German developed was in use in the Frankish domains which reached their first flowering under Charlemagne. But it was not until Martin

Luther translated the Bible into his own language that High German became stabilised. In Luther's Bible the German of today is clearly recognisable.

The origins of the words *Deutsch* (German) and *Teuton* (which came to be used in a collective sense of Germans generally), are obscure, though according to experts (e.g. Hugo Moser in *German Language History*) they are both probably derived ultimately from the early Latin word *Theodiscus*. It became in time *Teudiscus* and later in its Middle High German form *Diutsch*. The words Teuton and Teutonic appeared in the English language. The form *Teutonisch* (Teutonic) remained in German, though it is little used. Moser dates what he calls *Vordeutsch* (pre-German) from the second half of the fifth century until about 750, when it was followed by *Frühdeutsch* (early German) until 1170. Then came Middle High and Middle Low German until about 1500, when the High German was given by Luther the permanent form still in use.

There are many minor regional variations of present-day German, but the purest or standard form is spoken in the Hanover area and on the stage as *Bühnendeutsch* (stage German). Those who speak with a regional accent, of which the most marked in West Germany are those of Swabia and Bavaria, are not, however, looked down on as people are in Britain who speak with a provincial accent. There is no language snobbery of the kind that can easily make it impossible for a Lancashire man to get certain kinds of job in London.

The language is relatively easily pronounced by English-speaking people, though with its three genders and inflections it has a difficult grammar. The requirement that the verb of a minor clause must go to the end, together with other rigidities of word order, makes further complications. It lacks the convenient accusative and infinitive construction, cannot elide the conjunction *dass* (that), and cannot drop, as English often does, the relative pronoun. It is thus less supple than English, though not so rigid as it was, since the spoken language of today tends to be rather more flexible than the strict rules allow. The written sentence tends also to be shorter and crisper than the ponderous one of the past. German is, however, still fond of long compound nouns which can easily run to a score of letters or more. A tram or trolley stop comes out in German as *Strassenbahnhaltestelle* (*Strasse*=street; *Bahn*=track; *halten*=to stop; *Stelle*=place). Numbers are also written cumbersomely in one long word, so that two thousand eight hundred and forty-five becomes *zweitausendachthundertfünfundvierzig*. In practice today it would be written in figures. The last two digits are also in the reverse of the generally used order (*fünfundvierzig*=five and forty), which is a source of endless confusion to foreigners. They find themselves unable to take down telephone numbers correctly, and easily misunderstand when prices are stated.

NATIONAL CHARACTERISTICS

The German people have been widely regarded—above all since the second half of the nineteenth century, when they fell finally under the leadership of Prussia—as militarist and aggressive. The crimes many of them committed during the Nazi period were, with the possible exception of those committed in Russia during the Stalin period, without parallel among communities claiming the name of civilisation. But Germany is also a land of thinkers, musicians, writers, scientists and inventors. The contribution to European and world culture and civilisation of Goethe, Kant, Lessing, Schiller, Bach, Beethoven, Dürer, Cranach, Robert Koch, Otto Hahn, Einstein and hundreds of others could hardly be surpassed by any country.

Whether the German people of the present generation are militarist and aggressive is a question often put, but there is no general agreement about the answer. There are some who insist that 'the German character' is essentially militarist and aggressive, and from this they draw the conclusion that, although defeated in two world wars, they would be quite capable of 'trying again.' Russian policy towards West Germany seems indeed to stem from such a view. The rulers of the Kremlin oppose German re-unification for no doubt a variety of reasons, but underlying them all is the conviction—real or pretended—that if allowed to re-unite they would again threaten world peace.

Others, who reject on principle all generalised judgments, whether favourable or unfavourable, oppose the view that 'the German character' is militarist and aggressive, just as they contest the view that 'the German people' as a whole bear the guilt for either or both the world wars. It is morally indefensible, this group will maintain, to condemn a whole people, and indeed self-defeating, as those quickly discovered who, at the end of the Second World War, demanded that Germany should be deprived entirely of industry, turned into an agricultural country and excluded for ever from the society of nations. To have followed such a course (this second group argues) would have been to fall to the level of the Hitler régime itself, which set out to reduce the entire Polish and Russian people to serfdom—so that they might serve the needs of the Nazi Master Race.

The question whether the Germans are militarist and aggressive can still arouse emotion. But a discussion of whether they are—as so often said—hard-working and thorough, more easily provokes amusement. Those people who are not noted for the love of hard work—and that is surely many—tend to look with kindly condescension on the industrious Germans. There is no doubt that during the years of reconstruction that followed the Second World War, they worked with enormous application. Many of them still do, though it is easy to exaggerate the 'industry' of the Germans. To what extent the regional differences in Germany account for differences in character as between, say, north and south, cannot easily be determined. Physical environment—flat lands and sea in the north and lakes and mountains in the south—no doubt plays a part, as it always does in the formation of character. A further influence is religion—mainly Protestant in the north, mixed in the middle part of the country (though the Rhineland is mainly Catholic), and Catholic in the south.

RELIGION

Since Germany is the country in which the Reformation originated, it is perhaps inevitable that the division between Catholics and Protestants should be more clearly marked than in other countries where both faiths are represented. At any rate it remains true that religious differences do impinge on most aspects of the life of the country, including politics. The word '*proporz*' (proportion) is used to describe the deeply-entrenched practice by which public offices of every kind are distributed with at least one eye on the religion of the candidates.

In pre-war Germany about one-third of the 69 million inhabitants were Catholic and about two-thirds Protestant. Protestants lived mostly in the north and east (of which much is in the separate state of East Germany since the post-war division), while the Catholics were mostly in the Rhineland and the south. The Jewish population numbered some 564,000 before Hitler came to power (1933), but was reduced by emigration and expulsion to about 280,000 by the time the war broke out. As a result of Hitler's deportation and extermination policies the numbers were reduced drastically to hardly more than a handful of survivors. Natural increase and the return of small numbers of Jewish people from abroad have brought the figures up to about 25,000.

One of the many changes brought about by the great influx of people from the Oder-Neisse territories and from East Germany (see Chapter I) was a shift in the distribution of the religious communities. Of the roughly 60 million population of West Germany, some 50 per cent are now Protestant and 45 per cent Catholic. The rest are Jewish or members of other faiths.

HISTORICAL LANDMARKS

The Germanic tribes who entered recorded history fighting,

sometimes on the side of the legions of Rome, and sometimes against them—and constantly against each other—were first welded by the Emperor Charlemagne into some approximation of 'unity.' But the territories this remarkable warrior-statesman inherited, and to which he added greatly by conquest, finally embraced very much more than any of the later 'Germanies' that history has known. Charlemagne, in fact, came nearer to creating a united Europe than anyone either before him or since. Starting in 768 (when he succeeded his father Pippin) with domains that included most of present-day France, Holland, Belgium and much of later Germany, he was master as well, by the time he was crowned in Rome on Christmas Day 800, of the Italian peninsula as far south as Naples, of part of Spain, and of vast Saxon and Slav lands in the east. But following his death in 814, the fateful Frankish system of inheritance was applied, which required the division of a father's inheritance among his sons. Thus Europe was divided by the Treaty of Verdun into the kingdoms of Charles in the west, of Lothair in the middle, and of Louis in the east. It was from the Middle and Eastern Kingdoms that modern Germany slowly and painfully emerged. The Alps made it impossible to retain the southern territories, so that Switzerland and Italy broke away during the course of the years and established themselves eventually as separate countries. In the north the natural barrier of the sea gave relative stability, but in the west where there were no natural barriers other than the by no means always effective Rhine, and in the east where there were none at all, the boundaries of the Middle Kingdom were pressed in or pushed out concertina-like, depending on whether the forces inside or outside were stronger. In the west the hotly-disputed Alsace and Lorraine went finally to France after the First World War, while the Saarland went some years after the Second World War to West Germany. But in the east all is still in doubt. It has never, throughout history, been easy to define the word 'Germany,' and it is now harder than ever. Poland and Russia insist that the German territories they acquired after the Second World War are rightfully and permanently theirs, and the Communist authorities of East Ger-

The Country and the People   29

many accept their claim. The West German official view is that final decisions must be left to a peace conference, and successive governments have pledged themselves solemnly never to attempt to change any of their frontiers by force.

The Western powers had been uneasy from the start at handing over German territory to Poland and Russia, and did so only at Russian insistence and (in the case of Poland) in order that compensation might be made for east Polish territories that were annexed by Russia. Even so, though the western allies agreed to favour at the peace conference the retention by the Russians of the small area they acquired in this way (the northern half of East Prussia), they reserved their final decision on the larger areas placed 'under Polish administration.'

These areas are usually referred to as the 'Oder-Neisse' territories because they lie east of the line formed by the Oder and Neisse rivers. They comprise the southern part of East Prussia, the eastern parts of the provinces of Pomerania and Brandenburg, and Upper and Lower Silesia. They had become 'German' during the centuries of Germanic expansion under the Saxon emperors who emerged after the final break-up of the Frankish empire of Charlemagne in 887. The question how long any given area that has been acquired by conquest must be held until the rights of the original inhabitants are extinguished and it passes finally into the possession of the conquerors, will be for ever disputed. It arose in the seventeenth century when New England frontiersmen pushed out into the territories of the Red Indians, and more recently when the Jewish people laid claim to lands they had not held for two thousand years. Similarly, Germans, except the present Communist authorities of East Germany, and Slavs never agreed about the ownership of Slav territories in eastern Europe that were colonised by Germans between the tenth and twelfth centuries. The aim was not only to acquire what a proclamation issued by Saxon princes and bishops described as 'land rich in flesh, honey, grain, birds and abounding in all produce of fertility,' but to spread Christianity among the pagan Slavs. The method used then, as later in many other places, was fire and sword, though it was by peaceful means that Otto of Bamberg, one of the best of German missionaries, converted the people of Pomerania and added their lands to those of the Saxon emperors.

One of the greatest of these—Otto I—marched to Rome in 962 at the request of Pope John XII, who crowned him Roman Emperor. Thus the idea of the ancient Roman Empire that had never quite gone from the minds of men was revived again, though in a form that had unhappy consequences for the development of Germany. The Holy Roman Empire, as this joint creation of emperor and pope was later called, was 'neither holy nor Roman nor an empire,' yet centuries of effort invested in it by successive emperors prevented Germany from developing, in the manner of England and France, into a homogeneous state ruled from a central point. It suited neither popes nor princes that the successor to the Roman Empire should adopt the hereditary principle which, as it developed in England and France, gave great stability. Thus the Saxons were succeeded by the Salians and then by the Hohenstaufens, and the Holy Roman Emperor was a wanderer whose capital was at times in places as far apart as Palermo and Prague. Some stability came when it became the practice (though never more) to elect the head of the house of Habsburg as emperor and to keep Vienna as the permanent imperial capital. But, unhappily conceived as it was from the start, and weakened by the early centuries of strife between popes and emperors, the Holy Roman Empire none the less continued its precarious existence until the Napoleonic wars, when on 6 August 1806 the Emperor Francis laid down the crown of Charlemagne and Otto I and declared it 'dissolved.'

If the Holy Roman Empire was an influence that delayed for centuries the emergence of a clearly-defined German state, the Reformation initiated by Martin Luther in 1517, when he nailed his ninety-five theses to the door of Wittenberg Church, led indirectly—via the Thirty Years War—to the utter fragmentation of such unity as had by then been achieved. The divisive influence of the Reformation itself is still felt in every phase of German public life (see above—Religion), and the wars ended with 350 independent political units or 'Germanies.'

The Thirty Years War (1618-48) is usually referred to as a religious conflict, though it was that only in the sense that Catholics were on one side and Protestants on the other. Basically it was a power struggle between those involved. The aim of the German Catholic princes allied to the French Cardinal Richelieu and the Protestant ones fighting with the Swedish King Gustavus Adolphus was, quite simply, the enlargement of their possessions. France aimed at breaking the power of the empire and of the Habsburgs, while Gustavus Adolphus wanted glory and perhaps the imperial crown for a Protestant monarch—himself.

Brecht's play *Mother Courage* shows the modern theatre-goer something of the appalling suffering and destruction caused, which was comparable in its day with that of the Second World War. It laid waste the whole of central Europe and put civilisation back by a century. It ended only with the exhaustion of all concerned and after five years of peace negotiations in the Westphalian towns of Münster and Osnabrück. The Peace of Westphalia, when it was finally signed, brought religious freedom to the Calvinist branch of Protestantism, but it also confirmed the infamous *ius reformandi* or 'right' of territorial lords to determine the religion of their subjects.

Germany lost 40,000 square miles of territory, and France gained a dominant position in Alsace-Lorraine which, in 1681, enabled Louis XIV to annex the imperial city of Strasburg. Switzerland and the Netherlands broke away from the Empire, and Sweden entrenched itself in northern Germany. German princes and territorial lords were given the rights of 'sovereignty,' including the right to make alliances, not only with each other, but with foreign powers.

As France, under Louis, exploited its new strength by expanding into western and south-western Germany, imperial armies, led by the great Prince Eugene of Savoy, were fending off Turkish advances in the east. But events were also shaping in the north-east that were to have a fateful influence on German history.

The Prussians (*Pruzzi*) had peopled the Baltic coast area during the period of early Germanic expansion, but they were not Slavs. They were brought into the German fold largely by the activities of the Teutonic Order—a militant Christian band of warriors, first formed to fight in the Crusades. The Grand Masters of the Order and their descendants ruled the Duchy of Prussia until a Hohenzollern inherited in 1618.

The first important statesman of this rising north German power was Frederick William, the Great Elector. During his rule (1640-88) he restored order to the war-ravaged territories he had inherited—roughly the East Prussia of today and parts of Brandenburg—and expelled the Swedes from Pomerania. He was a great administrator and wise statesman who, by welcoming the brilliant Huguenot officials, craftsmen, writers and others driven from France by Louis XIV, did much to prepare the way for the remarkable future of his country. His son became, with the consent of the Emperor, Frederick I, the first Prussian King, in 1701. Thus Frederick II (the Great) had sound foundations on which to build when, later in the eighteenth century (1740), he ascended the Prussian throne. By the time he died in 1786 he had fought many wars, including the Seven Years War in which he was succoured by British subsidies and supported by British Hanoverian armies. This enabled him to keep his French—and other—enemies occupied while the British drove the French from North America and established themselves in India. One of the other enemies was Austria—as the imperial Habsburg territories centred on Vienna were by now becoming. The scene was thus already being set in the eighteenth century for the great nineteenth-century duel between Prussia and Austria.

But the progress of the new state of Prussia, whose capital had become the former Brandenburg village of Berlin, was not to be continuously upwards. There were to be defeats at the hands of Napoleon and much and deep humiliation. At the battle of Jena in 1806, the Corsican crushed Frederick the Great's once glorious armies so thoroughly that they all but disintegrated. Prussia had 'fallen asleep on the laurels of Frederick the Great,' said Heinrich von Stein, the great statesman and administrator to whom Prussia and through her, ultimately, Germany owed recovery more than to any other man. It was he, serving under the Prussian King Frederick William II, Frederick the Great's nephew and successor, who brought Prussia resolutely and effectively back into battle against Napoleon, and it was his friend Blücher whose aid was vital to Wellington's victory at Waterloo. Frederick William dismissed him in 1808, and Napoleon outlawed him as an enemy of the Confederation of the Rhine that he had created from a number of German states as a sort of French satellite. But von Stein sought asylum in Russia, where he was received with the greatest honours. He became the friend and adviser of the Emperor Alexander, though he returned to Germany after the wars.

By the time that Napoleon had been consigned to St Helena and the Congress of Vienna had danced and worked, the vast number of German principalities had been reduced to thirty-nine—including the Free Cities of Hamburg, Lübeck, Bremen and Frankfurt. They were known collectively as the German Confederation. There was as yet no German *Reich*, no unified Germany governed centrally from a single capital. But in 1851 Otto von Bismarck was appointed Prussian delegate to the Diet of the German Confederation at Frankfurt, and that meant, though no one knew it at the time, that the last stage of the long road had been reached.

It was at Frankfurt that Bismarck soon reached one of the most far-reaching decisions of his life—that the Austrian or Habsburg Empire, as the Holy Roman Empire had in effect become, was the chief obstacle to German unity. There was no room for both a united Germany and an Austria within the same political framework, whatever it might be called. This decision led directly to the battle of Königgraetz in 1866, at which the imperial Austrian armies were defeated by Prussian forces led by von Moltke. The victory was decisive in a political as well as in a military sense. Austria had been supported in the field by most of the states of the German Confederation, who remained loyal to the imperial idea and totally rejected the upstart Prussia. After the battle, Prussia under Bismarck annexed Hanover, the state of Hesse, Nassau, the Free City of Frankfurt, etc., but left Bavaria, which had also fought for the Habsburgs, intact. Bismarck had no wish to destroy the Empire, as he could see no more suitable future for the amorphous Germanic, Slav and other peoples within it than under Austrian overlordship. In view of what has happened in that part of Europe since the final dissolution of the Austrian Empire in the First World War, there are many who think that Bismarck was not entirely wrong.

Prussia emerged from the war with Austria as a first-class European power, and a long step forward had been taken on the road towards Bismarck's final goal, which was German unity under Prussian leadership. Since war had shown itself to be the most effective of all unifying instruments, another one would not be unwelcome to Bismarck. An opportunity to promote one occurred over the relatively minor issue of whether a Hohenzollern prince should be allowed to accept the Spanish throne, to which he had been elected by the Cortes. The French, under Napoleon III, objected to this extension of German influence, but, in a series of remarkably unskilful diplomatic moves, gave Bismarck his chance. By quite unnecessarily making public—in the famous Ems despatch (so named because the Prussian King William was in Bad Ems at the time)—the facts about negotia-

The Schildergasse in Cologne—part of the local car-free shopping centre.

Modern German housing near Bad Godesberg.

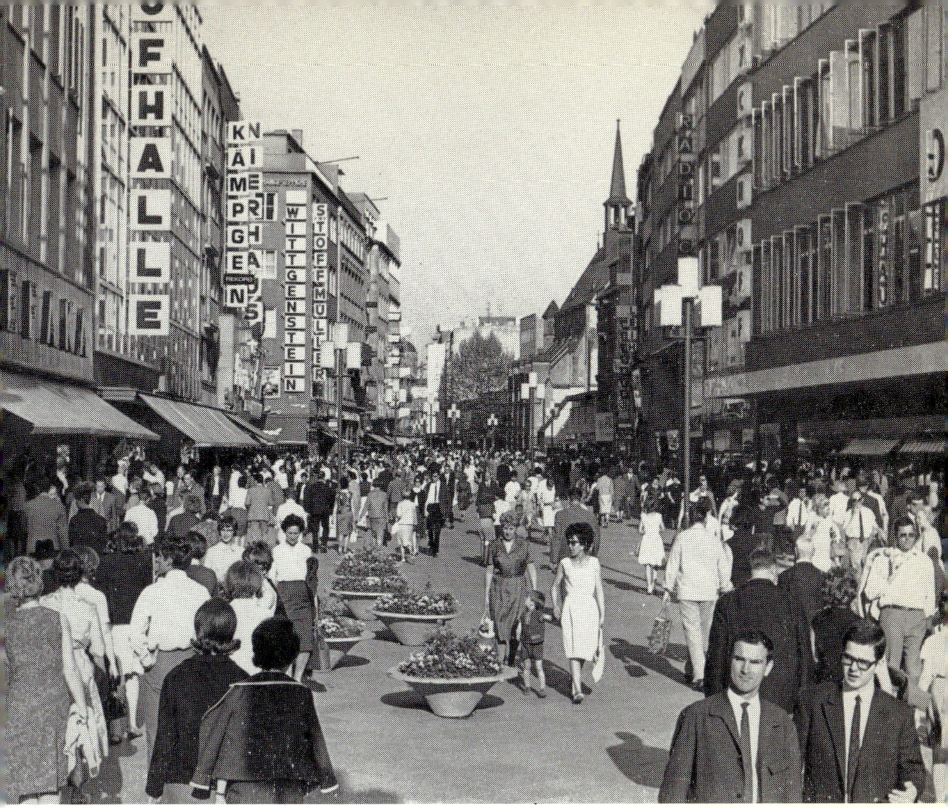
FHALLE
KÄMPGEN
WITTGENSTEIN
STOFFMÜLLER
RADIO

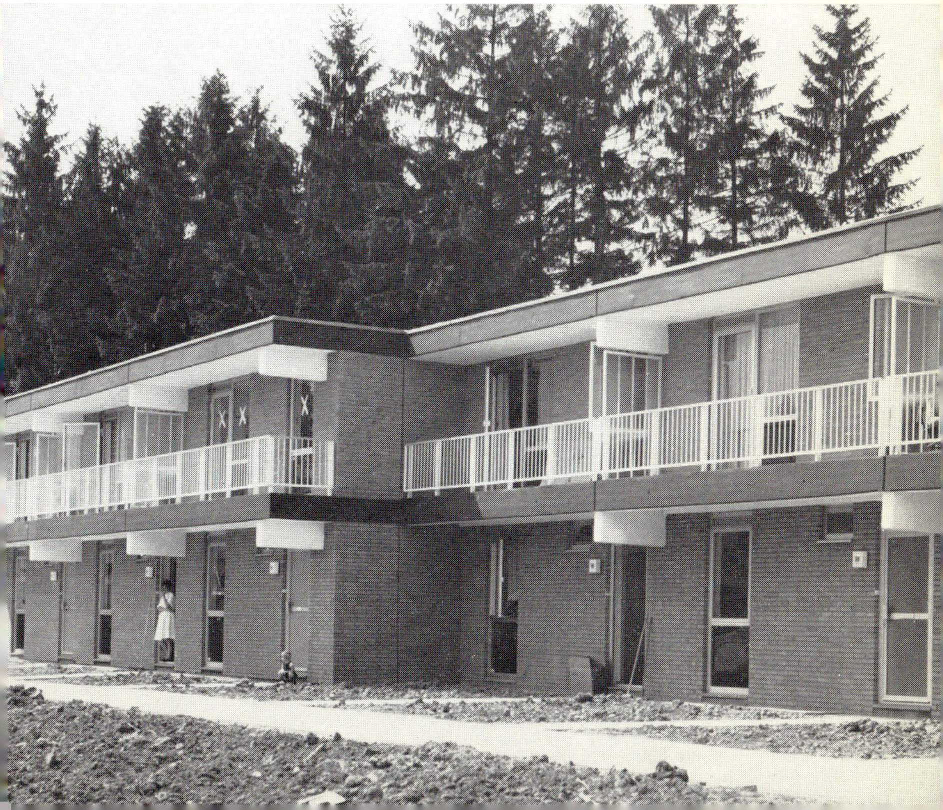

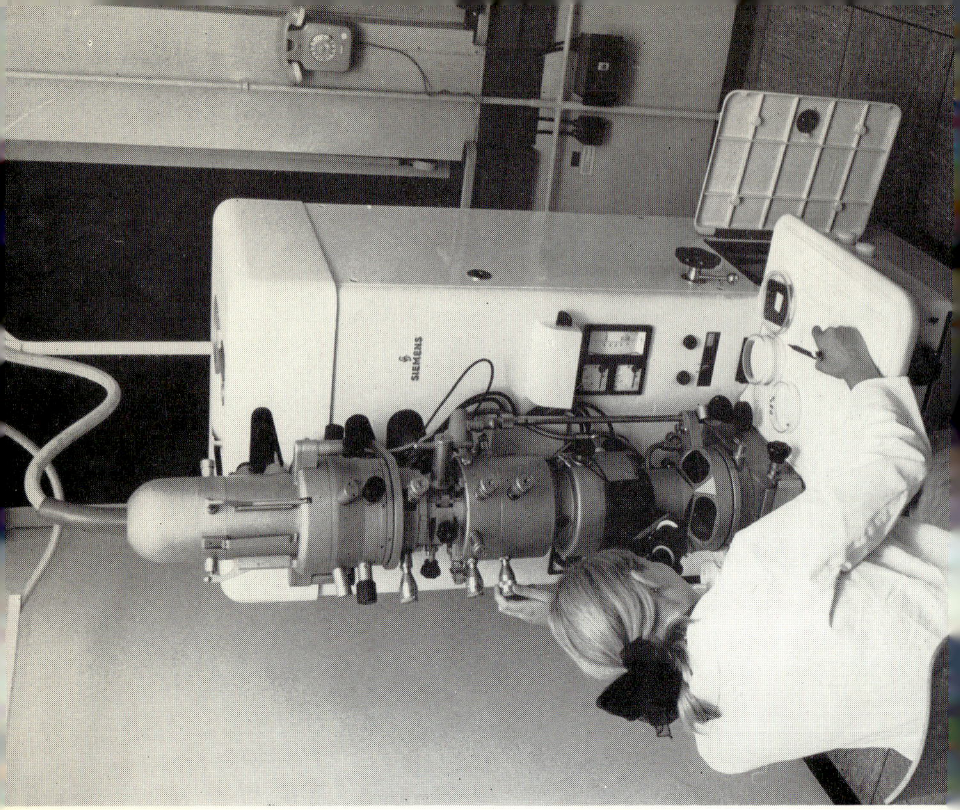

tions that would normally have remained secret, Bismarck pushed both sides to a point of no return. Relying, wrongly as it turned out, on what they believed to be their superior army, hoping, in vain as the event showed, for support from Austria and Italy, and being convinced that internal German dissension would continue, the French declared war on 19 July 1870. Being wrong on all counts—the south German states rallied at once to Prussia—the French were defeated and Bismarck's masterstroke was complete. He annexed Alsace-Lorraine and had King William of Prussia proclaimed German Emperor in Versailles. The south German states had agreed to this step in preliminary talks, and it was King Ludwig II of Bavaria who, at Bismarck's suggestion, took the initiative in offering the imperial crown to King William. The end of the road had been reached and the *Reich* was in being.

The course of German history had been, from the point of view of the unity and hence the political power and influence of the country, constantly erratic and at times disastrous. But it had advantages and benefits as well. Regional development led to the growth of great and splendid towns and cities that were civilised, cultured and famous throughout the world long before the late-coming *Reich* capital, Berlin, was anything more

---

Nuclear research in Jülich.

At work on a ship's turbine.

than a remote village. The independent princes left behind fine baroque palaces and theatres (see Chapter VIII) in Munich, Würzburg, Bamberg, Dresden and many other places, and many well-stocked museums and art galleries. This makes it possible for the visitor to find something worth seeing or hearing in every part of the country. Following the creation of the *Reich*, Berlin grew apace architecturally and culturally as well as politically, but it never dominated the country as London dominates Britain or as Paris dominates France.

Germany was now united as never before, though still not as completely as Britain and France, since its component states still preserved some considerable powers of local autonomy, and three of them—Saxony, Württemberg and Bavaria—even retained their own kings until the end of the First World War. It was left to Hitler to impose final—though brief—complete centralisation under Berlin.

Bismarck took the view that the new Reich was a 'saturated' state without territorial ambitions. But William II, who came to the throne in 1888 as a dashing and ambitious young man of twenty-nine, had other ideas. He dismissed Bismarck—'dropped the pilot,' as Sir John Tenniel pictured it in a famous *Punch* cartoon—and embarked on policies of his own. He wanted 'a place in the (African) sun' for his country, he wanted to break the bonds of 'encirclement,' and he wanted a navy that would rival Britain's. There are few British or other historians left who support the old propaganda thesis that Germany 'started' the First World War in the sense that the policies pursued by Germany under William II were its sole and direct cause. The more general view now—outside as well as inside Germany—is that, dangerous and irresponsible as German policies may have been, they were accompanied by follies and mistakes of both omission and commission on the part of all the countries concerned. 'The world slithered into war' is the current phrase inside West Germany.

The two unstable decades of the luckless Weimar Republic followed, and then came the Second World War, for which Germans are generally given and generally accept direct responsibility. By the time it ended Hitler was dead and his 'thousand-year *Reich*' was in oblivion.

The course of German history in the west since the war, has been set in the direction of political and economic reconstruction. This has meant a return to a form of government (see Chapter II) that recognises the regional history of the country and its firm linking to its former enemies in the west. West Germany joined NATO, and placed the whole of its newly-formed armed forces under NATO command, in order to support its new allies in facing threats from their ex-ally, Russia. Its main aim in foreign policy has always been the reunification of its divided territories, but to this has recently been added an attempt to improve relations with the Communist countries in eastern Europe, of whom two, Poland and Czechoslovakia, were brutally ravaged by Germany during the war, and of whom others were used as means to Hitler's ends.

As will be understood from what has been said about the Oder-Neisse problem, the two aims are, in the case of Poland at least, not entirely compatible, and there has in fact been less improvement in West German relations with that country than with any of the others concerned. East Germany is a separate case, since, in spite of the post-war division, it has not been incorporated into any non-German country. The West German Government would nevertheless gladly include it in their efforts at easing tension, but they meet with no response and are likely to meet with none as long as they find the price of recognition of the Communist régime there too high. Indeed, relations between the two parts of Germany tend to deteriorate rather than improve as the East German authorities feel themselves increasingly isolated in eastern Europe as a consequence of West German policy. This was undoubtedly one of the reasons that led them to give such eager support to Russia in the invasion of Czechoslovakia in August 1968. Indeed, there was good reason to believe that they played a not unimportant part in bringing about the Russian decision to invade. The invasion certainly put an abrupt end to the tentative steps towards better relations between West Germany and Czechoslovakia.

2

How the Country is Run

WEST GERMANY was constituted as a state in 1949 under the official title 'Federal Republic of Germany,' though its sovereignty was not fully restored by the occupying powers until 5 May 1955. It was formed from the territories occupied at the end of the war by America, Britain and (later) France. The constitution or basic law was drawn up by the leaders of new or reborn political parties and by legal experts under the chairmanship of Dr Adenauer, and was federal in character. This was required by the then occupiers, who believed that the relatively weak central government implied in a federal system would be less likely to attempt any fresh aggression, but was also in accordance with German tradition (see Chapter I—Historical Landmarks). The constitution provided for a president or head of state, a two-chamber parliament, a central or federal government, and state or *Länder* parliaments and governments. The number of these has grown since the fusion in 1952 of three south German states into one (Baden-Württemberg) and the re-inclusion of the Saarland (politically in 1957 and economically two years later). West Berlin occupies an anomalous position. West Germans like to regard it as an eleventh state, and as far as they can they treat it as such. But they are aware that under the Potsdam Agreement it is still—together with East Berlin—under four-power military government. Its status comes under discussion from time to time, as when the East German Communist authorities protest against the election there of the West German federal president, but there is no immediate likelihood of change.

Berlin will remain for some long time to come poised uneasily between east and west, with its eastern sector absorbed in practice, if not in law, into East Germany, while the western sectors are much less fully absorbed into West Germany than the West Germans would like. There is much local delegation of power by the three western powers to the local West Berlin authorities, but ultimate responsibility remains with them and in the last resort the West Germans know and accept this. They are aware that the security and freedom of West Berlin could not be maintained without the presence and power of America, Britain and France.

FEDERAL GOVERNMENT

The federal president is elected by a national convention (the *Bundestag* or Lower House of Parliament plus an equal number of representatives of the state parliaments) for a period of five years, and may be elected, at present, for not more than one additional term. The federal president exercises representational functions. He also signs treaties and accredits and receives ambassadors. He proposes the chancellor (head of the government) to parliament, but only after assuring himself that his nominee has a better chance than anyone else of the majority without which he cannot take or retain office. He appoints and dismisses cabinet ministers on the advice of the chancellor. The *Bundestag* is the direct representation of the people and hence the chief organ of state. It is elected in a secret vote by all citizens over twenty-one, for a period of four years. It has 496 members plus twenty-two from West Berlin, whose rights, however, because of the anomalous position of the city, are limited to speaking. They may not vote. The *Bundestag* has a president whose position is much the same as that of the Speaker in Britain, though he does not, like the Speaker, cease to be a party man when he takes office. He can and often does in practice play an important part in party politics. Deputies are technically free to vote as they please, but in practice they usually vote with their party or at most abstain. The *Bundestag* has a right to criticise and supervise the executive and to pass laws. It does this by a process similar to that in Britain—i.e. by a first, second and third reading of draft laws, and detailed examination in committee.

The *Bundesrat* is the second chamber in the West German parliament, as the House of Lords is the second chamber in Britain, and the Senate in America. But there the similarities are almost at an end. The House of Lords is traditionally not an elected chamber and, until the recent introduction of life peerages, was entirely hereditary. Members of the Senate are directly elected by popular vote, while members of the *Bundesrat* are appointed by the state governments from among their own members. The *Bundesrat* has the power to initiate laws (though in practice it rarely does) and laws initiated by the government must be placed before it before they go to the *Bundestag* (lower chamber). To facilitate compromise there is a mediating committee of eleven members from each chamber. It is called upon as required but sits in private. While the American states, whatever their size are each represented by two senators, the *Bundesrat* members are two, three or five from each state according to its population. They lack the freedom of members of the House of Lords and the Senate in that they are formally bound by the instructions they receive from the states they represent. The Senate's right to approve treaties and the appointment of ambassadors, etc., is quite unknown to the *Bundesrat*.

The federal government is led by a chancellor who chooses his ministers in general from members of the *Bundestag* who are also members of the party or parties to which he owes his majority. But—unlike Britain, though like America—cabinet ministers are not necessarily members of parliament. The first chancellor chosen under the constitution of 1949 was Dr Konrad Adenauer, who retained office at the head of a succession of governments for fourteen years. He was followed in 1963 by Dr Erhard and in 1966 by Herr Kiesinger. Under the constitution the chancellor has the right and the duty to lay down the main lines of policy on all subjects, and he can be removed

How the Country is Run 43

from office only by what is called a vote of 'constructive opposition.' This device was built into the constitution for the express purpose of making it harder to remove the chancellor from office than under the Weimar constitution, where it was so easy that the country was often for long periods without a government. The 'constructive opposition' clause means that the vote that removes a chancellor from office must at the same time appoint his successor. There can thus be no irresponsible dismissal of a chancellor by an opposition which is not agreed as to whom it will appoint in his place. The clause is one of the reasons for the great stability in post-war West German government. There have been none of the rapid changes that were familiar under the Weimar constitution in Germany and the Fourth Republic in France.

It follows that an adverse vote, except of the 'constructive opposition' kind, has no effect on the life of the government nor on any individual minister unless, as a consequence, he cares to resign or is dismissed by the federal president on the advice of the chancellor. The federal constitution court in Karlsruhe pronounces, when called upon, on whether or not any disputed law is constitutional, and it is the leading organ of the third power— the judiciary (see below).

POLITICAL PARTIES

In the first German parliament, elected in 1949, ten parties were represented. By 1961 the number had been reduced to three, and that figure remained at the 1965 election. There is some possibility that it will fall to two at the 1969 election, though it is more likely to rise to four. The reasons for these changes throw much light on the German political scene.

The Communist Party, which had fifteen members in the first parliament, gained too few votes to get seats in the second and was finally banned in 1956 as unconstitutional. A party was formed in 1950 (the BHE) from the ranks of the 12,000,000 refugees and expellees, specifically to represent them in parliament.

But so rapidly were the newcomers absorbed into the political as well as into the economic and social structure of West Germany that the BHE began to lose its significance. Its members later drifted into existing parties until the remnants merged (1961) with the somewhat nationalistic German Party. But this party gained no seats in that year's election and disbanded itself.

This trend towards a reduction in the number of parties has been hastened by a change in the electoral law made after the 1953 election. It was laid down that a party gaining less than five per cent of the total votes should get no seats at all. This has also prevented such new parties as have tried from time to time to enter the *Bundeshaus*, from doing so and has thus ensured, as was intended, that there should be no return to the multiplicity of parties that under the Weimar constitution made stable government impossible.

The three parties left are the Christian Democrat Union (CDU), which is here taken to include its Bavarian wing, the Christian Social Union (CSU), the Social Democrat Party (SPD), and the Free Democrat or Liberal Party (FDP). Of these, the CDU which is right-wing has emerged from every election so far as the largest party and has led every government. Once, in 1957, it had a clear overall majority and ruled alone, but otherwise it has always needed one or more partners in order to form a working majority.

The SPD has always been the second largest party, whose hopes of overtaking the CDU to take first place have constantly been frustrated. It is a left-wing party, but in an effort to pick up at least part of the middle-class vote that goes traditionally to the CDU it has in recent years thrown Marxism overboard. Unlike the British Labour Party, it has never favoured the nationalisation of industry. For a time the new image that it tried to create for itself in the early sixties brought votes in state elections, and in 1965 the SPD was quite sure it would win the federal election and break the hold of the CDU. Dr Adenauer, the great CDU leader, had retired from the scene, and Dr Erhard, who had succeeded him, was thought by the SPD to have no chance against their own candidate, Herr Brandt. But in the event it was Dr Erhard who won—by leading the CDU to first place yet again.

Like Dr Adenauer before him (in every year except 1957) Dr Erhard needed a coalition partner in order to complete his overall majority, and like Dr Adenauer (in 1953 and 1961) he formed a coalition with the FDP. But this always uneasy alliance broke up at the end of 1966, and a Grand Coalition, as it was called, of CDU and SPD took its place. This coalition of right and left had hitherto been thought impossible in federal politics, though it had been known before at state level, and came about only after weeks of hard bargaining. For the SPD it meant that at long last they emerged from opposition and took office—if only as junior partner to the CDU.

But from that time on until mid-1968 changes began to show themselves on the political scene that gave satisfaction to none of the three traditional parties. Angered, it seemed, by the disappearance under the Grand Coalition of an effective opposition (the only opposition party was the Free Democrats and they had only 49 deputies in a House of 500) the SPD and to a lesser extent the CDU began losing votes and the new extreme right-wing national party, the National Democrat Party (NPD), began gaining ground in state elections. Though they strongly objected to the description 'neo-Nazi,' the name continued to be applied to them and indeed there was no disputing that among its members there were a number of notorious ex-Nazis. The NPD overcame the five per cent hurdle in a number of state elections and finally had deputies in seven state parliaments. It seemed certain that it would get a number of seats—some estimates were as high as forty—in the federal election of 1969. This gave rise to discussion inside the CDU and SPD parties as to whether the electoral law should not be amended, along the lines of the British majority system, so as to make the entry of the small new party impossible. But unwilling as the two main parties were to face possible charges of 'manipulating' the electoral law to their own advantage, and facing as well the fierce opposition of the small FDP who under any British-style system would have been crushed, the two major parties hesitated. They abandoned the plan altogether when in late 1968 the NPD vote in Lower Saxony municipal elections sank from its earlier seven to eight per cent (in state elections) to hardly more than the minimum five per cent (the figure was 5.2 per cent). The hope was that the NPD had passed its peak in view of the unquestioned achievements of the Grand Coalition in many fields of policy, though above all in bringing the country out of the economic recession of 1966-7. An examination of the constitutional position showed that it might have been possible to deal with the problem of the NPD by banning it, as the KPD (Communist party) had been banned, but with the electors showing signs of withdrawing their favours from the right-wing extremists, the major parties no longer felt called upon to take action that in any event would have been controversial. An additional reason for refraining from any further extreme action against extremist parties was that, after much discussion among West German Communists, a new party was formed which, although unquestionably Communist, was not sufficiently close to the legal borderline for the authorities to feel called upon to take action. They felt strong enough at that stage to be able to take a tolerant attitude, and since the new party called itself not the KPD (*Kommunistische Partei Deutschlands*—the banned party), but DKP (*Deutsche Kommunistische Partei*) the matter was allowed to ride. The outsider may think that there was no more than a distinction without a difference between the old party and the new, but the whole political trend was at that stage towards greater liberalism, so, as the constitutional lawyers put them under no pressure the authorities felt they could relax. Thus the position in early 1969 was that, although there was the danger that the NPD might enter the next federal parliament at the election of September 1969, it was no longer so serious as it had been. It was improbable, if not quite impossible, that Communists would do so. The new party would indeed hardly be in a position to deploy candidates in time.

An altogether different and quite unorthodox phenomenon on the political scene from about mid-1968 onwards was the APO (*Ausser Parlamentarische Opposition*—Extra-Parliamentary Opposition) which, as its name implies, was not a parliamentary party. It was in fact the collective term used by student political rebels of a variety of kinds, whose motives ranged from a demand for reform of the antiquated German system of university administration to plain anarchy. Many of the students (with beards, uncut hair and rag-bag clothing) seemed to aim at nothing less than dismantling the entire political and social system and replacing it by—they did not seem quite sure what. They demonstrated, like so many of their contemporaries in other countries, against the Vietnam war or against anything else that seemed to them to be reprehensible. They called themselves the Extra-Parliamentary Opposition because they were opposed to all the existing parliamentary parties and indeed to parliament itself. The official ring of the title seemed to many to give the students a standing that they had not (or not yet) acquired, but many politicians were finding it right and worthwhile to take them seriously and to discuss political and social problems with them.

LOCAL GOVERNMENT

There are variations in the system of local government within the states, arising in part from German tradition and in part from the occupation years, when the occupying powers tended to impose their own national system. These again have in some cases been changed by the German authorities. There is thus much variation of both title and function in different parts of the country. The state itself is divided into a number of districts (*Regierungsbezirke*) with a president (*Regierungspräsident*) appointed by the state at the head of each. All other local government units are subject to varying degrees of supervision and control by the *Regierungspräsident*. The states have in effect much greater control over the units beneath them than the federal government has over *them*. They, for example, have considerable influence through the *Bundesrat* on the federal government in Bonn, but the local government units have no corresponding organ through which they can influence the states.

In the larger and relatively independent towns there is in the old British zone an elected and honorary lord mayor (*Oberbürgermeister*), and a chief town clerk (*Oberstadtdirektor*) who is appointed by the town council as a paid official. Whatever their size and whether *kreisfrei* or not, all towns have their elected town council (*Stadtrat*). But the smaller towns, together with villages and parishes (*Gemeinde*), are grouped into *Landkreise*—very roughly, counties—which have their own local parliament (*Kreistag*). At the head of the *Landkreis* in the old British zone is the *Landrat* (representational) and the *Oberkreisdirektor* (administrative). The first is honorary and the second paid.

Outside the British zone the norm is that the representational and administrative functions are combined in one elected and paid office—*Oberbürgermeister, Landrat*, etc.

These differences as between the former British zone and the rest of the country persist right down to the *Gemeinde* (parish or borough) which is the lowest unit of local government administration. Each *Gemeinde* has its own elected council (*Stadtrat* or *Gemeinderat*) and its own representational and administrative offices, usually combined but sometimes separate. At the head of the *Gemeinde* is the *Bürgermeister, Stadtdirektor*, etc.—there are many variations of title. Under the states (which exercise control through the *Regierungspräsident*) the *Gemeinde* have many responsibilities connected with schools, roads, libraries, museums, theatres, etc.

THE MINISTRIES

The federal government includes not only such ministries as are familiar in most other countries—foreign affairs, interior, defence, finance, etc.—but several that may well be entirely unknown elsewhere. Among them is the Ministry of Refugees and Expellees, formed to look after those millions of people referred to in Chapter I who were driven, after the war, from their homelands in what had been the eastern part of Germany, or who had left voluntarily in order to escape from the Communist system established there by new masters. The numbers still arriving have for the reasons mentioned in Chapter I declined from a flood to a small trickle, which reached in 1968, however, the figure of 32,660. There is thus still work for the ministry, dealing with the newcomers as well as settling the claims of earlier arrivals which the law enables them to make (see Chapter IV). But the decline in the importance of this ministry is in part a measure of its success. That a country so battered and chaotic as West Germany was at the end of the war, should have been able to absorb and re-settle such a vast inflow of population, without a major political and social upheaval, is an achievement less well known in the outside world than that of the 'economic miracle' but in its way no less remarkable.

Also a consequence of the break-up of pre-war Germany is the Ministry of All German Affairs. Its task is to do nothing less than to 'seek ways and means of ending the division of Germany,' but, since this division cannot be ended without the consent of the victor powers who brought it about, there is in practice only a limited field of activity for the ministry. What it can and does do is keep a constant eye on the political, economic, social and other consequences of the division and, besides alleviating them where it can in the present, make contingency plans for the day of reunification whenever it may come. It seeks to keep alive in the public mind the idea of reunification, and to this end works together with the non-party organisation known as the Curatorium for Germany Indivisible. It concerns itself with the many kinds of individual and family hardship that arise from the division of the country, and proposes, where appropriate, to other federal or local authorities, the kind of relief measures that might be suitable.

The family is seen in West Germany as the basic unit of the entire social edifice, and the Family and Youth Ministry was set up to concern itself with the problems of the family as such. In practice this has meant that the ministry has played a leading part in bringing about the legislation which provides the allowances for children described in Chapter IV (Social Security). The ministry also studies tax problems as they affect the family, social and housing questions, and all matters affecting property rights as between husband and wife. Its executive powers are limited, but it can and does make recommendations to other authorities on these and other subjects. It co-ordinates or assists where it can in providing marriage guidance or advice and in securing special aid, holidays, etc., for such needy members of the family as, for example, overworked mothers with large families and limited income. It concerns itself particularly with youth problems, including education, post-school training, welfare and sport. The ministry has also been instrumental in securing the construction of special holiday-homes for families, of which there were, by the end of 1968, 114 in the country with a total of 13,500 beds. More are under construction.

THE CURRENCY

The present West German currency—the *Deutschemark* (DM)—was introduced on 20 June 1948 to replace the hopelessly-inflated *Reichsmark*, whose circulation had risen in ten years from 6.4 to 72.5 thousand million (see also Chapter IV—How they Live). There are people still alive who remember taking *Reichsmarks* by the sackful to the baker to buy a loaf of bread. The new rate was fixed at £1=DM11.76 and $1=DM4.20. But such was the economic boom that followed, that the DM was revalued in March 1961 to £1=DM11.20 and $1=DM4. The British devaluation of November 1967 left a rate of £1= DM9.60 while the dollar was unaffected. There are day-to-day variations in these basic rates in accordance with supply and demand on the international exchanges. The volume of money in circulation at the end of 1965 was DM31,450 million (£2,810 million=$7,860 million) of which DM2,000 million (£180 million=$500 million) was in coin and the rest in notes. After small variations since then, the figures were in early 1968 roughly the same.

The currency is based on the decimal system, with the DM divided into 100 pfennigs. Notes are issued for DM5, 10, 20, 50,

100, 500 and 1,000, with coins for DM 1, 2 and 5. Pfennig coins are in units of Pf 1, 2, 5, and 10.

At the end of 1958 West Germany, like most west European countries, made its currency fully convertible and, unlike some of the others—e.g. Britain, it has maintained full convertibility ever since. This means that holders of DM can exchange them in any quantity into other currencies and move them freely into or out of the country.

Convertibility applies equally to current and capital transactions and to the sale of gold, which is unrestricted on the home market (it was suspended for a few days only during the 'gold rush' of early 1968). Gold may also be imported and exported freely. Although no new gold coins are minted in West Germany, the gold coinage of other countries, both new and old, and including that of both Britain and America, is offered for sale by the banks.

The DM has thus become one of the world's hardest currencies and it inspires great confidence both at home and abroad. Indeed such is the fear of the German people of inflation (they lost their savings after both world wars) that no government which allowed the value of the currency to fall by more than a minimal amount could hope to remain in office. The loss of value of the DM from its 'birth' in 1948 to its twentieth 'birthday' in 1968 was in fact 26 per cent, compared with 29 per cent for the American dollar and 52 per cent for the pound. It was the hard DM, above all else, that enabled West Germany to take a leading part so often in supporting sterling in its various crises, and in aiding the French franc in November 1968.

The confidence of the West German people themselves in their currency is shown by the way they have—in spite of their two earlier disastrous experiences—begun to save again (see also Chapter IV—How they spend their money).

TAXATION

There is nothing new about tax payers' dislike of *paying* taxes but it is not often that tax collectors object to *collecting* them. Yet this was the situation in West Germany in 1968, when the League of Tax Payers and the League of Tax Collectors issued a joint declaration. It drew attention to the fact that there were fifty different taxes in West Germany, and insisted that the number could be reduced to twenty-five without loss of revenue to the authorities. The tax payers were prepared to admit the 'regrettable necessity' of paying taxes, and the collectors were prepared to collect. But both sides called for rationalisation of the system.

The complications of the tax system in West Germany are—like so much else in the country—largely a consequence of its federal character. The federal authorities, the state authorities and the *Gemeinde* (small town and village) authorities all have power to levy taxes and all make good use of them. They vary from the old turnover tax (since 1 January 1968, in accordance with Common Market requirement, the added value tax) which is levied on all goods sold, from ships to sealing wax, and all services rendered, e.g. by tax advisers, hairdressers, etc., to the tax on dogs. The added value tax goes entirely to the federal authorities and is its largest single source of revenue. In 1967, when it was still the turnover tax, it amounted to just one-third

---

A potter at work.

A glass school in Cologne.

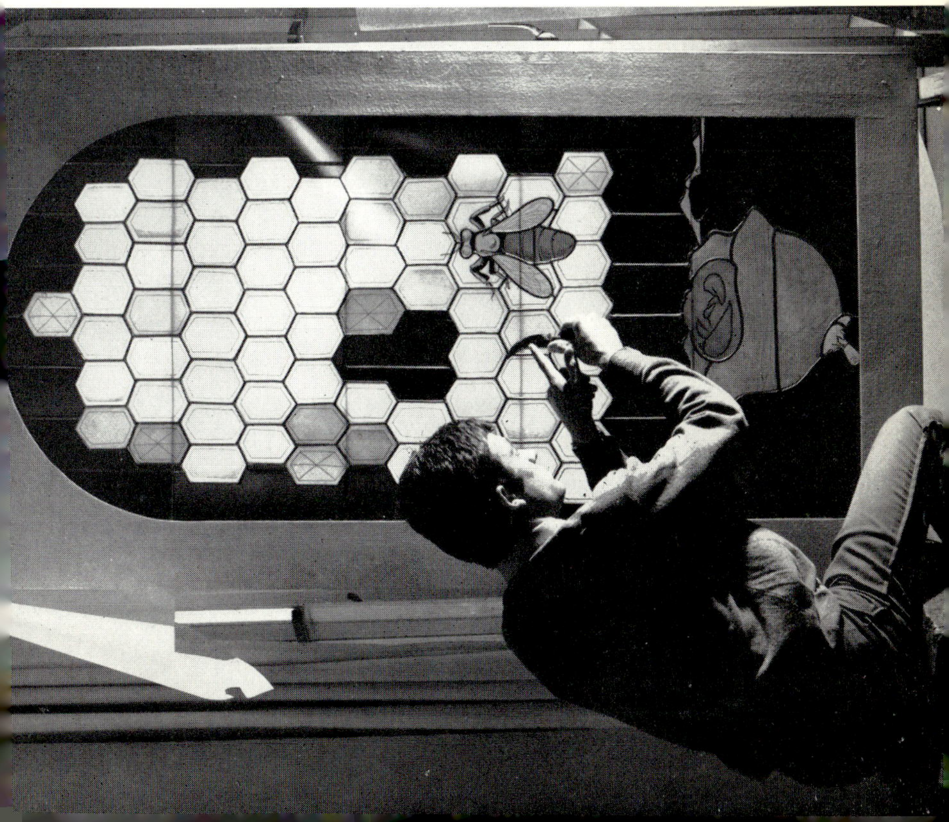

of the total federal revenue, which was £6,820 million=$19,250 million. The total tax revenue of federal and state authorities taken together was in 1967 £8,910 million=$24,750 million. The public debt of the same authorities at the end of the same year was £9,630 million=$26,750 million.

The largest single source of revenue (about 40 per cent) in the state as a whole is in West Germany, as in most highly developed countries, the income and corporation tax. But in West Germany this tax is divided between the federal and state authorities (who pass on varying parts of their shares to the *Gemeinde* authorities) in proportions that have varied between 35 per cent and 39 per cent, though they were fixed for 1967 and 1968 at 37 per cent. Each side tries hard to get the biggest possible share, and the annual process of dividing the cake is usually preceded by acrimonious debate between the federal and state authorities. The two per cent difference that is usually involved amounts, after all, to some £90 million=$250 million.

Other taxes that flow exclusively into the coffers of the federal authorities are the turnover equalisation tax (on imports), customs duties of all kinds, and the special levies on tobacco, coffee, sugar, brandy, sparkling wine, mineral oil, etc. The turnover equalisation tax (now renamed the import equalisation tax)

Oil and Chemical works between Bonn and Cologne.

Steelworks in Dortmund.

ensures that imported goods do not escape the turnover (now added value) tax on goods produced at home. As it will continue to be levied now (post-July 1968) that inter-European Community customs duties have been abolished, it will be one of the irritating items contributing to the feeling that customs barriers have not been abolished after all. Whether the amount an importer pays is called 'customs' or 'import equalisation tax' is liable to seem to him academic. The amount charged is based on an estimate on what the turnover (added value) tax would have been if the goods had been produced in West Germany.

The state authorities levy property tax, motor vehicle tax and beer tax for their exclusive use. The *Gemeinde* authorities levy taxes on dogs, playing cards, etc., and sometimes on drinks (mainly soft) which are then usually charged as a separate item on restaurant bills. The annoyed guest who does not understand why he should be charged *Getränkesteuer* (drink tax) in one restaurant and not in another will be told that it is imposed by the *Gemeinde* he happens to be in at the moment.

The burden of taxation has risen steadily and now absorbs about 35 per cent of the gross national product. This compares with 10 per cent in 1913. Per head it is about £224=$629, which makes West Germans among the highest taxed people in the world. In Britain 31 per cent of the gross national product is taken by taxation and in America 28 per cent.

Income tax is levied at progressive rates which reach 53 per cent at the top, compared with 96 per cent in Britain and 70 per cent in America (not including the 10 per cent surcharge introduced by President Johnson in 1968). Of those liable for income tax some 90 per cent pay at the rate of 20 per cent, but over eight million employees pay no direct tax at all.

A special feature of the tax system of West Germany is the states equalisation scheme, devised and put into force in 1955. The need for it arose from the fact that, since some of the component states of the federation are more populous and richer than others, any given tax will yield correspondingly different amounts. Yet the financial responsibilities may, under some headings (e.g. resettlement of expellees and refugees), be greater in the poorer than in the richer states. Thus the scheme provides a pool into which the richer states (e.g. North Rhine-Westphalia and Hamburg) pay money, while the poorer states (e.g. Bavaria and the Saarland) draw money from it.

POLICE

The differently-coloured uniforms of West German police (e.g. green in North Rhine-Westphalia and blue in Bavaria) are an outward and visible sign that they are under the state authorities. The federal authorities have no police force of their own, though there are provisions under which, in times of grave and widespread disorder, they could, in consultation and with the consent of the state or states concerned, take over the police. Such an emergency has never so far occurred. The total force numbers some 75,000 men.

But as well as the *Schutzpolizei*, as they are called, whose duties are the normal ones of traffic control and general maintenance of public order, there is a special force of some 10,000 men known as 'stand-by' police (*Bereitschaftspolizei*). These men are quartered in barracks, are armed with grenade-throwers and light machine-guns, and are in effect a para-military formation. They perform none of the duties of the *Schutzpolizei*, but are held in reserve for states of emergency. They are distributed throughout the states and are mainly financed and administered by them, though with some financial assistance and supervision of training from the federal authorities. Formally they are also under state control, though there is no doubt that—again in consultation with the states—the federal authorities would take them over in the grave kind of emergency for which they are provided.

The powers of the federal authorities to act in times of emergency, including war and civil war, were greatly extended by legislation finally passed, after ten years of heated political dispute, in 1968. But the basic control of the police by the states was not affected.

There is a second para-military force known as the Frontier Defence Force. It was set up by, and is controlled by, the federal authorities mainly because of the east-west division of the country which leaves open the ever present possibility of encroachment or infiltration from East Germany. The West German authorities would not wish to confront such action with their army, and so have provided what is something of a half-way stage. The hope is that the Frontier Force would be able to keep action from the east below the level of full-scale civil war. In the former British zone a purely British frontier service, on a very small but highly-organised scale, acts as an additional buffer. It is invariably first on the scene when the East Germans make small but constant pin-pricking encroachments, so that the Frontier Defence Force has never been seriously engaged.

The responsibilities of the Frontier Defence Force, which is some 20,000 strong, extend 19 miles inland, but should invasion threaten it can be used throughout the federal territory. As well as constantly patrolling at the east-west border, it is used for passport-control duties on the strictly international frontiers. The force is armed in much the same way as the *Bereitschaftspolizei*, and like them is accommodated in barracks.

There is also the criminal police (*Kriminalpolizei*) which, as the name indicates, concerns itself mainly with crime. It is a plain-clothes force under the control of the states, although a federal office at Wiesbaden acts as national and international intelligence-collecting centre. This force also has a special security section in Bonn, whose task is the protection of important national and international personalities. On such occasions as the visit of the Queen, the late President Kennedy and General de Gaulle, its duties have been very heavy. The force as a whole and the security section may be roughly compared with Britain's Scotland Yard and the Special Branch.

JUSTICE

The judicial system is of the 'continental' type, and is thus very different from the 'Anglo-Saxon' system of Britain and America. While, for example, a trial in Britain and America takes the form of a duel between prosecution and defence, in which the judge intervenes only as umpire and speaks at length only in his summing up at the end, the judge (or president of the bench of judges) plays from the start the leading part in a West German court. It is he who interrogates both the accused and the witnesses *before* handing them over to prosecution and defence counsel for cross-examination. Nor is the judge's interrogation limited to the offence that is before the court. It will cover the whole previous life of the accused and, at the judge's discretion, of the witnesses. It will include also reference to a matter that in Anglo-Saxon courts is most rigidly excluded. A routine question to the accused is always '*Sind Sie vorbestraft?*'—have you any previous convictions against you?—a question that at the start of proceedings is inconceivable in a British or American court.

It is thus seen at once that the rules of evidence are very different in the two systems. It might almost be said, indeed, that in the West German system there are no rules of evidence. Hearsay, opinion and everything that has any bearing on the trial is freely admitted, though the importance, if any, attached to it is naturally a matter for the court to decide. The offence known as contempt of court prevents the naming of suspects in the British press. But West German law recognises no such offence. Thus persons believed or suspected or assumed by the press to be guilty of a crime are named in the newspapers, not merely before they have been tried and convicted, but before they have appeared in court or indeed before they have been arrested or even named by the police as suspected or wanted. Such devious phrases as 'the police were tonight questioning a man they believe may be able to help them,' are therefore unknown in West Germany. The papers are likely to say the 'the murderer XY was tonight questioned by the police.'

While the law as applied in Britain derives in a complicated way from ancient common law, from the case law interpretations based on it by the courts over a period of centuries, and from the relatively recent volume of statute law passed by a succession of parliaments, West German law derives with much greater simplicity from the great civil, criminal and commercial law codifications of the late nineteenth century. These legal works endeavoured to strike a balance between what might be called ancient Germanic tradition and the Roman law which, especially from the sixteenth century onwards, found increasing acceptance. The codes were twisted and distorted, and in large part done away with altogether during the Nazi period, but have now been brought back with certain amendments and additions in the field of criminal law.

A separate and additional system of administrative courts (*Verwaltungsgericht*) has also been set up to ensure that the individual citizen shall never again be subjected to the arbitrary acts of the executive as he was under the Nazis. These courts make it possible for the individual to appeal against the decisions of officials, e.g. in matters of taxation, the compulsory selling of private land for road building etc., in a simpler and more direct way than is possible in either Britain or America. The administrative courts play a most important part in protecting the freedom of the press and the rights of the individual to express and disseminate opinion, his rights of assembly and inheritance, etc.

A system of social courts (*Sozialgericht*) watches over the rights of the individual as derived from social legislation—pension rights, etc.—and labour courts (*Arbeitsgericht*) protect him similarly in connection with trade-union law, the right to proper notice of dismissal, paid holidays, etc.

The final appeal from all West German courts is always to the corresponding Federal Court (civil, criminal, administrative, etc.). There is also a Federal Constitutional Court whose task it is to watch over the constitutionality of all legislation, administration and justice. It is separate from all other organs, and had no counterpart in pre-war Germany. It has been called upon to make a number of decisions that have been of the greatest importance—for example, in ruling that the Communist Party was unconstitutional and therefore incapable of continued legal activity. All justice, except in these federal courts, is in the hands of the state authorities.

The court of first instance for both civil and criminal proceedings is the *Amtsgericht*. It is followed by the state court (*Landgericht*) and Higher State Court (*Oberlandesgericht*). The Higher State Court can act as a court of first instance when cases involving treason or conspiracy are transferred to it from the Federal Court. Both the *Amtsgericht* and the *Landgericht* sit in criminal matters, usually with two lay judges or *Schöffen*, as well as, usually three, professional judges of whom one is president. At the *Landgericht* there is a panel of jurymen (*Geschworene*) in the more serious cases—e.g. where death is involved. All these are state courts.

With the exception of labour courts of first instance, representation by counsel is always assured and there is a right of appeal right through to the Federal Court except in cases where the *Oberlandesgericht* has acted as court of first instance. The independence of judges is guaranteed by the constitution—a fact that has caused the authorities embarrassment in a number of cases when judges found to have a politically dubious, though not criminal, past could not be removed from office. A great mass of Nazi legislation was abolished at the end of the war, either by the occupying powers or later by the West German authorities. The death penalty also went, so that the heaviest penalty is life imprisonment. It can be imposed for murder, high treason, certain forms of treason, genocide and the preparation of war of aggression. These last two cases seem to show a praiseworthy attempt by West Germans to learn from their experiences under the Nazis. Proceedings for dealing with criminal cases have long been under review, and detailed measures have been prepared for modernising and humanising them, especially with respect to the methods used for dealing with psychopaths, neurotics and perverts. The new arrangements, when they come into operation, will provide for less repressive measures for dealing with the criminally inclined who are not criminal addicts, the number of short prison sentences will be reduced, and the probation system much extended. The criminal code affecting young persons will be radically overhauled.

THE NAZI LEGACY

In the legal, as in every other field of West German life, the Nazis left a heavy legacy. Thus much of the time of the courts is given to applying the laws which seek to make good some of the losses inflicted on Jews and others during the Nazi period. Within the framework of the federal restitution law, a total of 3,389,000 individual claims were made, and by the end of 1965, 3,113,916 of them had been settled. A total of some £2,886 million=$7,826 million had been paid out from resources provided by the federal and state authorities, and an estimated further £1,310 million=$3,675 million will be required.

But as well as payments to private persons, the West German state made a reparations agreement with the state of Israel under which it undertook to deliver goods to the value of £270 million=$750 million. The goods were intended to help the newly-born state in its gigantic task of assimilating the large numbers of Jews driven by the Nazis from their homes in Europe. The agreement had been carried out in full by 30 June 1965. A further £40 million=$110 million was placed by the West German authorities at the disposal of the Jewish Conference as a special 'hardship fund' to be used on behalf of Jews who had been persecuted by the Nazis but who were living outside Israel.

NAZI CRIMINALS

While most of the leading surviving Nazi criminals were dealt with by the allies at the Nuremberg and other trials, many thousands of greater and lesser wanted men had either found it easy to assume a new identity in the chaotic early post-war years and go underground in their own country, or to escape abroad. As soon as they were given permission by the occupy-

How the Country is Run

ing powers, the newly-constituted West German courts dealt with a number of cases, but large numbers were still outstanding. A cry was raised in the outside world that the West Germans were deliberately 'dragging their feet'—that they were out to allow the Nazi criminals to escape justice. But the truth was that West German justice was operating under severe handicaps. First, since it was in the hands of the states, it lacked the central co-ordination that was needed to trace the missing men. Some clues as to their whereabouts might reach the hands of the authorities in each of two or more states, but there was no machinery for pooling the knowledge. Secondly, vast quantities of documents relating to the Nazis and their crimes had been seized by the allies at the end of the war and removed to their own countries.

Finally, in 1958, a central agency was set up by the state authorities in Ludwigsburg. Its task was to co-ordinate the work of tracing wanted Nazis, and to seek documentary evidence and find witnesses able to testify in the courts. It had no power to originate legal proceedings, but handed over the evidence it collected to the state authorities for action. From then on much progress was made. The task was vast, but lawyers working in the central agency were tireless in visiting America, Poland and other countries where documents were held, and in seeking out witnesses who were often survivors of concentration and death camps. The witnesses were often scattered even more widely than the documents across the world, but many of them were finally brought together for the great Auschwitz trial of 1962-4 and others.

The allies sentenced a total of 5,000 persons found guilty of complicity in Nazi crimes, 806 of them to death. By 1967 the West German authorities had carried out enquiries in 73,793 cases and had sentenced 6,179 persons. Enquiries are still being made in some 20,000 further cases.

But the question of the 'further cases' has proved a very difficult one. Under the statute of limitations, which in West Germany applies to murder as to other offences, no action against persons against whom it had not yet been initiated would normally have been possible after 1965. But the prospect of this raised such an outcry, both inside and outside West Germany, that after much public discussion and heated parliamentary debate the twenty years was extended by four. Failing further extension the time limit would have run out at the end of 1969, but eventually the two coalition parties agreed on a compromise. The SPD wanted a complete abolition of all time limits on the prosecution of murder of every kind, whether Nazi or not. The changes finally agreed with the CDU abolished all time limits on genocide and extended the time limit for murder (of every kind) and in part for complicity in murder, by a further ten years from the end of 1969. It was the difficulty of defining the word 'complicity' that caused the lawgivers to leave a gap which the prosecuting authorities will be called upon to fill. If the complicity should, in the eyes of the public prosecutor, be of sufficient minor character, or should the alleged offender have acted 'under orders,' then he may escape. But there would be no escape for such notorious wanted men as Martin Bormann and 'Gestapo' Müller and others against whom proceedings on major charges have long since been opened.

LAWYERS

All law students take the First State Examination, but they cannot practise until they have also passed the Great State Examination and completed two-and-a-half years of practical training. They can then choose whether to become a defence lawyer, a public prosecutor or a judge. There is no distinction in the profession as in Britain, between solicitor and barrister. All lawyers may plead in all criminal courts, but in civil cases only in the court to which they have become accredited.

THE ARMED FORCES (*Bundeswehr*)

Following defeat and the disbandment of the *Wehrmacht*

(defence forces), West Germany was for eleven years without any armed forces. But on joining NATO in 1955, and after recovering its sovereignty in the same year, West Germany undertook to set up a *Bundeswehr* (federal forces) as a contribution against the threat of Russian aggression. A gasp of horror went through the world at the thought of a rearmed Germany, but in the view of responsible western statesmen there was no alternative. However, the Bonn government, led by Dr Adenauer, agreed to place the whole of the *Bundeswehr* under the control of NATO. West Germany is still the only country whose entire armed forces are commanded by NATO. After rejection by the French of the plan for a completely integrated European defence force this was the best solution that could be found.

But if there was little welcome in the outside world for the rearmament of West Germany, there was none at all among the ordinary West German people. They had had so much of war and soldiering and even uniforms that after 6,000 volunteers had entered barracks on New Year's Day 1956 to form the nucleus of a new army a great '*ohne mich*' (without me) movement grew up among the young men who knew that they would shortly be called up for eighteen months' military service.

In spite of this West Germany had, by the end of 1966, met its commitment to place twelve army (*Heer*) divisions, a smaller air force (*Luftwaffe*), and navy (*Kriegsmarine*) units under NATO command. The total strength of the federal forces at the end of 1967 was 460,000 men, of whom 287,000 were army, 98,000 air force and 33,500 navy. The rest were in a territorial force under national command, limited to duties inside national territories. Of the total force, 222,000 are regulars.

The army is made up of seven armoured infantry divisions, three armoured divisions, one mountain division and one airborne division. Besides conventional weapons, which include the West German-built Leopard tank with the British 105 mm gun, the army has the American-controlled Sergeant and Honest John nuclear weapons.

The air force has the nuclear-armed Starfighter, and the navy has three nuclear destroyers under construction in American shipyards, but as with the army all nuclear weapons are under American control. The West German government has voluntarily renounced the right to produce or acquire any ABC (atomic, bacteriological or chemical) weapons of its own. It has scrupulously kept to its undertaking in this matter, and that is one source of its hesitation in signing the non-proliferation treaty.

The air force comprises five heavy bomber squadrons, three light bomber squadrons, two heavy and one light reconnaissance squadrons, and battalions with Pershing and Hawk ground-to-air rocket missiles.

As well as three nuclear destroyers on order, the navy has three destroyer squadrons, five minesweeper squadrons, one escort squadron, five fast patrol-boat squadrons, one minelayer squadron, one coastal patrol squadron, one fleet utility squadron, five naval air squadrons, one naval air rescue squadron, one landing craft squadron and one submarine squadron.

The national Territorial Defence Force has six military district commands with subordinate regional districts, signals, ordnance, engineering and medical corps.

For reasons of national economy the defence budget was fixed in 1966 at £1,550 million=$4,350 million, which was £89 million=$250 million less than in the previous year. But in 1967 it rose by £178 million=$500 million. This was 26.7 per cent of the total national budget. It came second only to expenditure on social security at 33.5 per cent.

Every year the federal military procurements board concludes contracts for about £540 million=$1,500 million. This makes it Europe's largest purchaser. Of the total some £375 million=$1,050 million are spent at home and £160 million=$450 million abroad.

3

The Regions

THE STATES that comprise the West German Federal Republic all have a character of their own, but their boundaries are not in all cases historical. This is a result in part of the east-west division of pre-war Germany and in part of the exigencies of the post-war situation in West Germany, when the occupying powers who were then responsible felt themselves obliged to pay more attention to the creation of viable administrative units than to history. Yet, in spite of all this, Bavaria and the two Hanseatic cities of Hamburg and Bremen derive directly from history. Berlin is a special case, as has already been indicated.

BAVARIA

The Bavarians were one of the original Germanic tribes and they have, despite all the admixture of the centuries, retained a clear identity of their own. It is often said of them, if indeed they do not say it themselves, that they are Bavarians first and Germans afterwards. They are different from the 'Prussians,' as they tend, quite inaccurately, to call all Germans but themselves, and they enjoy being different and insist on being different. As one example: in the rest of West Germany the big right-wing party that has been dominant in politics since the war bears the name Christian Democratic Union, but in Bavaria it is the Christian Social Union. Most of the time this is a distinction without a difference, for the two normally vote together in the *Bundeshaus* and in general behave as if they were one party. But most of the time is not all of the time, and this means in practice that, when feeling in a particularly Bavarian mood, the Christian Social deputies will at least threaten to vote their own way. And since in politics a threat is often enough, they sometimes either get their own way or at least compel the larger Christian Democrat group to compromise. In 1966, when a new chancellor was chosen in succession to Dr Erhard, it was the clannish Bavarians who, by voting in a forty-nine-strong block, turned the scale in favour of Herr Kiesinger and against Dr Schroeder, who was the alternative candidate.

Bavaria has been throughout the centuries an agricultural area, and because of its green fields and forests, its lakes and mountains, a great tourist attraction. It is still all that and much more; a land of glorious baroque architecture and of people who love and cultivate their old costumes and customs—their green *loden* cloaks, their leather shorts and their folk dancing. The Bavarians are also a race of most formidable beer-drinkers, and they brew it in an innumerable variety of ways. There is beer brewed from wheat as well as from barley, and there is smoked beer and a succession of *Bock* ('goat' beers for some reason) which are stronger than the rest and produced at various seasons of the year. And in the *Hofbräuhaus* in Munich they have the most famous beer-drinking house in the world.

But the Bavarians are well aware that in the twentieth century they cannot live on either agriculture or tourism alone. They already had the great engineering firms of Krauss-Maffei and MAN, which is associated with Britain's Rolls-Royce, and the Bavarian Motor Car Works, which produces fine cars, but these are not by themselves enough. Bavaria has therefore seized on the opportunities presented by the great expansion of the industries based on oil, and, with supplies coming up from Genoa by pipeline, is turning the town of Ingolstadt into a great refining centre. Big electro-technical firms like Siemens are also expanding their already considerable installations in Bavaria, and the small but growing aircraft industry is largely centred there. West Germany's first atomic reactor was built in Bavaria, and that alone

The Regions

is an important pointer for the future. But whatever it has done and may yet do in this direction, Bavaria is aware that the great industrial heart of the country is, and will always be, in the distant Ruhr area which has always tended to look towards its French, Dutch and Belgian neighbours in the west, and to the sea in the north, for its food and other supplies and its trade. This has all been intensified by the development of the Common Market, about which the Bavarians are not nearly so happy as most of the rest of their fellow-countrymen. They are therefore putting much effort into developing commercial and cultural ties both with Italy in the south (Milan is not so far from Munich as Bonn, the federal capital, or Düsseldorf, the industrial capital), and above all with Czechoslovakia and the countries of the Danube basin. To this end they opened in 1968, in their fine old town of Regensburg, a new university that will specialise in cultural ties with eastern and south-eastern Europe, and they are doing all they can to hasten completion of the great Rhine-Main-Danube canal which will permit ships to travel from Rotterdam to the Black Sea. They publish with satisfaction from time to time figures showing the great increase of trade on the sections that are already complete. (See Chapter VII—Waterways.)

Bavaria is in area (27,239 square miles) the largest of the West German states, though with a population of rather more than ten million it comes well after the much smaller North Rhine-Westphalia, which includes the Ruhr industrial area. Some two million expellees and refugees have been absorbed by Bavaria since the war, but the population remains mainly Catholic (over 70 per cent). Because of its geographical position, it has always been a link between Germany and the south and east, and that tie is underlined by the mixture of nationalities found there. Of the many guest workers who come into West Germany from Italy, Jugoslavia, Greece, Turkey, etc., some 200,000 remain in Bavaria.

Of the many fine cities in Bavaria, the capital, Munich, has become something of a substitute capital for the entire country. Bonn is too small ever to be anything more than the political and administrative headquarters of the federal government. Young people from all over the country tend to gravitate to Munich, as in other countries they go to the capital. In Munich they find a university and a lively cultural and intellectual life. They have also, in Schwabing, something of a German version of the left-bank area of Paris. The state government of Bavaria is in the hands of the Christian Social Party, though some of the towns, including Munich, are ruled by the Social Democrats.

LOWER SAXONY

What is left of the great historic land of Saxony proper lies in East Germany. But the Lower Saxony created in 1946 as a *Land* or state of what later became the Federal Republic of Germany is none the less well entitled to its name. If not as the governmental and administrative unit that it is today, Lower Saxony has existed since the middle ages as the name of an army corps district. The present state includes the old Saxon 'imperial city' of Goslar, which, with its still well preserved imperial palace, is now a tourist attraction that should not be missed, and so is *Braunschweig* (Brunswick), where a splendid statue of a

---

Production of Volkswagen cars at the main works at Wolfsburg.

Liquid Gas containers at Hamburg.

lion recalls the Saxon archduke Henry the Lion. After the overthrow in 1180 of that great warrior by the emperor Frederick Barbarossa, the area disintegrated dynastically and territorially so that it cannot and does not claim anything like the historic and racial coherence of Bavaria. As well as its Saxon inheritance, Lower Saxony includes the provinces of Oldenburg, Schaumburg-Lippe and Hanover—which was annexed by Prussia for the part it played in aiding the Austrians in 1866. It remained Prussian until 1946, when the four victor powers, in perhaps their only act of common accord, dissolved Prussia entirely and removed its very name from the map.

In Lower Saxony, perhaps more than in any other state of the federation, the problems and absurdities created by the east-west division of Germany are revealed. The east-west border is for some 350 miles (half its total length) the border of Lower Saxony, and it is from the Lower Saxony town of Helmstedt that the foreign traveller to Berlin by road or rail enters East Germany. In passing it may be said that he would be well advised to go by air from nearby Hanover, since the formalities, and still more the delays, often imposed by the East German authorities can be extremely frustrating. Air travel involves no contact at all with the East German authorities, and hence no

---

Tractors are rapidly replacing oxen and horses on German farms.

Gathering grapes for wine in the Palatinate.

special formalities, such as acquiring a visa and paying road tolls, or delays. Near Helmstedt the border can also be seen as it divides an area of brown coal deposits into two and so renders exploitation on both sides difficult and largely uneconomic. The areas of Lower Saxony, and the other states involved, adjoining the east border are a permanent problem to the authorities, since industry and commerce tend to avoid them.

In area Lower Saxony is, with 18,296 square miles, the second largest of the West German states and in population (6,732,000) the fourth largest. The population includes some two million expellees and refugees, and re-settling these has imposed considerable strain on the resources of the state. These are in any case poor compared with those of North Rhine-Westphalia and some other states, and Lower Saxony is one of the receiver states under the equalisation of revenue scheme (see Taxation). But poverty is a strictly relative term, and neither in Lower Saxony or anywhere else in West Germany does it have any resemblance to what still exists in parts of southern Europe.

In fact there is much agriculture (over 70 per cent of the population still live in rural areas), some natural resources—oil, potash, iron ore—and much highly developed industry. Hanover, the capital of Lower Saxony, is an important centre for rubber manufacturing, mainly tyres, and electrical and other industries, and the great international industrial fair is held there every year. Elsewhere in the state almost the whole range of capital and consumer industries is represented, with the great Volkswagen motor car works at Wolfsburg at the head of them. Volkswagen is the biggest commercial enterprise in West Germany and the biggest car works in the world outside America. Included in Lower Saxony are the smaller, North Sea ports of Emden, Wilhelmshaven, Cuxhaven and others, which the authorities develop as far as they can, though they are aware that they can never compete with Hamburg, Bremen and Bremerhaven. The coastal area of Friesland offers great attraction to those tourists who like a quiet, green countryside, and there is also the chain of small islands on some of which no cars are allowed, though there is plenty of garage room for them on the mainland. The splendid hill country of the Harz lies only partly in Lower Saxony, since the east-west border runs through it.

In contrast to Bavaria, nearly 80 per cent of the population of Lower Saxony are Protestant. The state governments are coalitions, though led by the Social Democrats as the largest party.

BADEN-WÜRTTEMBERG

Most of the state boundaries drawn after the war on the basis of history and hit-and-miss proved satisfactory enough, if not ideal, but in the south-east three of them proved too small to be viable and were amalgamated, after a referendum in 1952, into the present Baden-Württemberg. Even now the historic differences between the two component parts are such that Baden has separatist notions and may, after a new referendum, break away.

Division is in fact even more familiar to this part of Germany than most. The Swabian tribes of this area produced in the twelfth century the great Hohenstaufen family which, after bloodthirsty wars with the rival Welf or Guelph family, established itself as a new line of emperors. Their lands became the centre and heart of the Holy Roman Empire and their Frederick Barbarossa (Red Beard), partly because he was a great man and a great emperor, and partly because his mother was a Welf, brought peace for a time. But Frederick's military excursions into Italy, and his renewed disputes with Saxony's and Bavaria's Henry the Lion, undid all, and fragmentation of the area followed. More than anywhere else in the country, small independent cities and territories, secular and ecclesiastical, appeared and lasted, with variations, for centuries. As well, however, there was great intellectual development in the area, and the universities of Heidelberg (1386), Freiburg (1457) and Tübingen (1477) were established.

Germany's first technical college was founded at Karlsruhe, in what is now Baden-Württemberg, in 1825, and a second one appeared in Stuttgart, the capital of the state, four years later.

These two institutions helped to give the area the leading position in industry which it has since retained. Though it lacks raw materials, it is more highly industrialised than any other state in the federation, including North Rhine-Westphalia itself (with the Ruhr). Some 20 per cent of all industrial workers in the country live in Baden-Württemberg, and produce some 17 per cent of its industrial turnover. Germany's prestige Mercedes cars and its famous Porsche sports cars are produced in the Stuttgart area and elsewhere in the state are great electrical firms such as Bosch, and more recently electronic and computer concerns have appeared and flourished. One of West Germany's greatest chemical combines is in Ludwigshafen. But there are also over 300,000 farms in the state, producing a wide variety of agricultural produce, including wine which, though not so famous as those of the Rhine and the Moselle, is none the less very good.

Baden-Württemberg is third in size in West Germany, with an area of 13,803 square miles. It is third also in population—about eight million. This is some 14 per cent of the total population of the country, a fact which, taken with the figures given above, underlines the industrial development of the state. It borders on Switzerland and France, from both of which it is separated by the Rhine, and even though it lacks such striking natural scenery as the Alps of Bavaria, it is none the less one of the most beautiful of the West German states and is also singularly rich in varied and splendid cultural monuments.

It includes among its scenic glories the great area of the Black Forest which is as popular as ever with the tourist. But there are also the quiet charms of the valley of the river Neckar, with its innumerable hilltop castles (some now hotels), and the Oden Forest which, if not so well-known as the Black Forest, is still very popular with those who know it. There are also many spa resorts, including Baden-Baden, the most famous of them all (see also Chapter VIII). In the south the Rhine flows into the great *Bodensee* (Lake Constance) from Switzerland and out again, first west and then north on its long journey to the sea. Steamers ply on the lake between Baden-Württemburg, Switzer-

The Regions 77

land and Austria, and there is much of interest to the visitor on its banks. In the town of *Konstanz* (Constance) the building in which the famous Council was held in 1417 is still well preserved.

The government of Baden-Württemberg is, since the 1968 elections, a coalition of the Christian Democrat and Social Democrat parties. As one of the richer states it pays into the equalisation fund.

NORTH RHINE-WESTPHALIA

The present state of North Rhine-Westphalia is formed from the two old provinces of Lower Rhine and Westphalia—which from the end of the Napoleonic wars onwards were Prussian. In earlier centuries the area had been a tangle of principalities that had developed in much the same way as in south-west Germany and for the same reason—the overthrow of the Saxon Grand Duke Henry the Lion by the Emperor Frederick Barbarossa in 1180. The British occupying forces performed their part of the agreement to break up Prussia in 1946, and they set up North Rhine-Westphalia in the place of the part of Prussia that was in their zone. Since then the two provinces have for the first time in history been governed as a single political unit.

Although only fourth in size (13,119 square miles) among the federal states, North Rhine-Westphalia has, with 16,195,000 inhabitants, by far the largest population, including about 3,500,000 expellees and refugees.

Of the more than seven million people employed in all branches of the economy, nearly two-and-a-half million are in the traditional mining, iron and steel and power industries of the Ruhr, which is the heartland of the state. Among the workers were, at the peak in the early sixties, some 400,000 foreigners, but this number declined during the recession of 1966-7 to 300,000. It is now tending to rise again. Total industrial production in North Rhine-Westphalia stands at three times its pre-war level, and its domestic product accounts in all for nearly one-third of the national total.

The state owes its early industrialisation and its later rise to economic predominance to its vast deposits of coal and its smaller ones of iron ore (see Chapter I). But the exploitation of these, and the development of great industries based on them, were much facilitated by favourable communications, especially by the Rhine which, via Duisburg, the biggest inland port in Europe, and other great riverside towns, gives a direct link to the great seaport of Rotterdam and through it to the world.

Although coal, iron and steel and the heavy industries associated with them are traditional to the Ruhr and still of the greatest importance, modern technological development has made it possible, and indeed necessary, for the area to widen the base of its economic structure. Thus it is now the newer but fast-growing chemical industry and oil refining, with supplies by pipeline from the north German port of Wilhelmshaven and from Rotterdam, which enable the Ruhr to remain the greatest industrial centre, not only of the country, but of Europe. But diversification has led also in North Rhine-Westphalia to the growth of glass and synthetic fibre industries, of plastics, textiles, finished clothing, food production and much else besides.

Yet this should not be allowed to give the impression that North Rhine-Westphalia is nothing but a vast, industrial black-country. On the contrary, laws against pollution have done much to clear the air of the Ruhr, and apart from that the far-flung state includes, south of Bonn, a good deal of the finest scenery of the Rhine valley. There are also within the state borders such historic towns and cities as Charlemagne's Aachen (Aix-la-Chapelle) and Cologne which, besides its not very distinguished cathedral and Eau-de-Cologne, can lay claim to being certainly for the British, the Dutch and the Belgians, the gateway to West Germany. Düsseldorf, the capital of the state, has recovered from wartime destruction to become one of the most modern and flourishing cities in Europe. In Münster the room can still be visited in which, in 1648, the Treaty of Westphalia was signed that at last put an end to the disastrous Thirty Years War.

Rather more than half the population of North Rhine-Westphalia is Catholic, and the government is a coalition led by the Social Democrats but including some Free Democrats. As one of the richer states of the federation, it pays into the equalisation fund from which the poorer states draw.

SCHLESWIG-HOLSTEIN

Schleswig-Holstein is the most northerly state of West Germany and the natural link between that country and Scandinavia. Indeed, the two duchies, as they once were, were united for over 400 years, from 1460 to 1863, in the person of the king of Denmark. They were annexed by Bismarck on behalf of Prussia in 1866 'without a jot or tittle of historical or legal claim,' as H. A. L. Fisher wrote in his *History of Europe*. After the First World War a strip of the area north of Flensburg went, after a referendum, to Denmark, while after the Second World War Schleswig-Holstein became for the first time in its long and troubled history a separate political unit, with all the powers of local self-government that its status as a state of the West German federation implied. Its small Danish minority is represented in the state parliament, and after some early uncertainties it no longer counts as a serious problem.

Schleswig-Holstein is, with an area of 6,045 square miles, one of the smallest West German states (only the city states and the Saarland are smaller), and its population density is, at 389 to the square mile, exceeded in every state except Lower Saxony and Bavaria. But so many of its inhabitants in the early years after the war were expellees and refugees (1.2 million out of a total of 1.5 million), that it became known as 'the poorhouse of the Federal Republic.' Only systematic resettlement of the newcomers from the east made it possible to reduce their numbers by about a third. But in spite of this Schleswig-Holstein remains a mainly agricultural state and hence still something of a poor relation. Small quantities of crude oil, and shipbuilding yards in Kiel, Rendsburg and Lübeck, aid the economy, but the state will never be rich. It is one of the receiving states under the financial equalisation scheme.

This does not, however, mean that Schleswig-Holstein is not immensely attractive to the visitor. Most people find farmland and green fields more agreeable to the eye than factories, and they make up the greater part of the area. Inland the state is full of forests and lakes which, with their fishing, bathing, sailing and other facilities, make excellent holiday country and there are also the two seas—North Sea and Baltic—with scores of delightful resorts. From many of these there are connections by sea to Scandinavia, while road links are being constantly improved. The projected deepening of the Kiel canal will make this already important link between the North Sea and the Baltic able to take modern shipping. A road tunnel under the canal was completed in 1961, while the road-travel time between Hamburg and Copenhagen has been cut by two hours since the completion in 1963 of the magnificent 'Birds' Flight Route,' which includes a bridge over the Fehmarn Sound and a ferry service from the German island of Fehmarn to the Danish island of Laaland. Kiel, which is the capital of the state, has, besides its shipyards, a university, and is famous for its annual regatta.

Schleswig-Holstein is predominantly (88 per cent) Protestant, with a government that since the early occupation years, when it was Social Democrat, has always been a coalition led by the Christian Democrats.

HESSE

The state of Hesse was formed in 1945 from the former Prussian provinces of Kurhesse and Nassau, the provinces of Starkenburg and Upper Hesse, and the part of the province of Rhine-Hesse which is on the right bank of the Rhine. The part of this province on the left bank of the river was incorporated into the state of Rhineland-Palatinate. The great industrial town of Frankfurt on the Main is the biggest in the state, but the spa town of Wiesbaden on the Rhine is its capital. Besides much industry (electro-technical, rubber, etc.), Frankfurt has Germany's biggest airport which, after London and Orly, is the third largest in Europe. It handled some eight million passengers in 1967, and is constantly expanding. Frankfurt is also the home of the Federal Bank, and as a consequence the most important financial centre in the country. The great autobahn junction, where east-west and north-south routes meet, is a masterpiece of road planning and construction. The town was badly battered during the war, but its historic buildings—one where emperors were once crowned and another where Goethe was born—have been splendidly restored. In Frankfurt also is the famous Paul's Church, where an abortive attempt to establish a liberal constitution for Germany was made in 1848 and where President Kennedy spoke during his visit to Germany in 1963.

The landscape of Hesse is most varied—from the Hohe Meissner hills to the Rhine, from the valley of the Weser to that of the Neckar, and from the rather bleaker hills of the Vogelberg to the woodlands and hills of the Taunus, the Odenwald and the Spessart. Industry and agriculture are well balanced and, under a ten-year Great Hesse Plan, the state government is trying to make further improvements—by decongesting thickly populated industrial areas, etc. Hesse has an exceptionally large number of the health resorts and spas at which most of the ills to which man is liable can be treated. Wiesbaden, the capital, is the largest, but Bad Homburg and many others are famous.

Hesse possesses considerable resources of soft coal, potash, crude oil and natural gas, while expellees and refugees have brought with them from the east such new activities as the glass industry and the fur trade. Book publishing has also become of great importance in the area of Frankfurt, where the German book fair is now held. Kassel, Fulda and Hersfeld are important industrial centres, while the gentle Rheingau produces the finest of the Rhine wines. The reason for their exceptional quality is that here for a short stretch the Rhine runs east and west, so that the vines get more sun.

Protestants are, with some 64 per cent of the population, in the majority in Hesse, but both religious confessions have deep historical roots in the state. St Boniface, the Apostle of the Germans, is buried in Fulda Cathedral, while Philip the Magnanimous was one of the early supporters of the Reformation. In Marburg Castle Martin Luther and the Swiss reformer Huldrich Zwingli held their famous disputation. The government of Hesse has, except for a brief early period, always been led by the Social Democrat party acting either alone as at present or in partnership with others.

HAMBURG

Hamburg is West Germany's biggest port and, with a population of 1.8 million, its second biggest city after West Berlin, which has 2.2 million. But it is also a state within the federal republic—with a proud history that goes much further back than that of Berlin. It is small in size compared with all its fellow states except Bremen and Saarland, but with its 290 square miles it is none the less five times as big as the independent principality of Liechtenstein. It lies on the estuary of the Elbe, sixty-five miles from the open sea, at a point where at the beginning of the ninth century the Emperor Charlemagne and his army made a crossing. It was fortified in about 825 and became an archbishopric in 835. The Emperor Barbarossa laid the foundations of the later fortunes of Hamburg when, in 1189, he granted freedom of tolls 'between sea and city.' In 1216 the local commercial and ecclesiastical interests combined in a solemn agreement that their city was 'forever one and should have one council, one council chamber and one court of law.' It became then what it has remained virtually ever since—a city state.

Its first golden age was as a leading member of the Hanseatic League from the thirteenth to the fifteenth century. After the discovery of the New World it became a port of transhipment for goods from North and South America, and in time for trade with Africa and the Far East. That is the function it still discharges, with the valuable aid of the free port facilities deriving from Barbarossa and retained with difficulty in 1881 when the German Customs Union was formed. These facilities mean that ocean-going ships can begin to discharge on arrival without customs formalities and goods may be stored, processed and repacked for re-shipment without paying customs duties.

Hamburg's harbour occupies about one-seventh of the total area of the city and, since reconstruction after wartime bombing, has become as modern and efficient as any in the world. It handles all types of shipping from great passenger-liners to bulk and mixed cargo freighters of every kind. But for all the advantages of its position, it lacks water that is deep enough for the largest modern vessels, especially the big, new tankers. This hampers it in competition with Rotterdam, though it has great plans for deepening the Elbe and even constructing further port facilities closer to the sea. Another problem for the port of Hamburg has been created by the iron curtain across Europe, which means that goods to and from the east, including Prague, now use the East German Baltic ports. Communications, even with its own hinterland, are not as good as they need to be, so that goods travelling to and from West Germany's industrial Ruhr tend to go via the Rhine and Rotterdam. This problem is to be tackled by the construction of a great new north-south canal linking the Elbe with the existent canal networks of the interior.

The centre of Hamburg lies delightfully round the Alster lake, which is connected by the Alster river with the Elbe. There are pleasant public gardens on the banks, and water buses chugging up and down provide a pleasing alternative to more conventional forms of city transport. Bridges separate the outer from the inner Alster, round which are fine shopping streets, great hotels and all the appurtenances of a big city. Near by are the *Planten und Blomen* botanical gardens, the opera house, theatres and much else of interest.

With a tax revenue of £352 million=$968 million, it is one of the richer states of the federation, and it contributes £39 million=$107 million to the fund from which financially weaker states are helped. It is a traditionally Social Democrat stronghold, though other parties have at times shared in the government. The city parliament is known as the citizens' council, and the city government, elected by the council, as the senate. Unlike most of the rest of the states which have a minister-president at the head of the government, Hamburg has a mayor.

BREMEN

The former Hanseatic town and port of Bremen on the estuary of the Weser, and the port of Bremerhaven some forty miles closer to the mouth of the river, form together West Germany's smallest state. They have an area between them of only 156 square miles and a population of only 750,000, of which 150,000 are in Bremerhaven. Like Hamburg a 'city-state,' Bremen has a long and proud history which also goes back to Charlemagne. It was he who, after the local people had first slain missionaries sent to convert them, set up a bishopric there in 787. Like Hamburg, it owes much to the great Barbarossa who granted it basic civic rights in 1186. From these derive the traditional independence of Bremen, which at the Congress of Vienna was given separate membership of the German confederation.

Although one of the lesser North Sea ports compared with Rotterdam, Antwerp and its West German sister, Hamburg, Bremen, and especially Bremerhaven, are of great importance for transatlantic passenger liners. The great American liner *United States* (53,000 tons) is constantly seen there, as well as West Germany's own passenger flagship the *Bremen* (32,500 tons), and many others. Bremen is the main port of entry for a number of important bulk cargo goods including tobacco, grain, coffee and copper. Deep-sea fishing is also an essential part of the economy. Bremen played a rather special rôle in the early years after the war as the port of entry for supplies to the American occupation forces who, in their south German zone, had no access to the sea. It thus became an American enclave in what was otherwise in those years the British zone. Proud of its standing as a 'gateway to the world,' Bremen has an overseas museum which specialises in displays illustrating life in the Far East, in the Pacific etc. But it has many other attractions for the visitor, including its famous *Rathaus* (city hall) whose Gothic main structure was given a renaissance façade in the seventeenth century. Below it is the old *Ratskeller* (restaurant), with a wine list that claims to be the longest in the world, and with old wood carvings and wall paintings well restored. Outside the *Rathaus* stands the famous 'Town Musicians' monument—a cock standing on the back of a cat which stands on the back of a dog on the back of a donkey. The monument derives its name from the fact that the four animals are all in their various ways giving tongue.

Like Hamburg, Bremen is a traditional Social Democrat stronghold. The yield from taxes is at about average rate, so that it neither contributes to nor receives from the tax equalisation fund.

RHINELAND-PALATINATE

The state of *Rheinland-Pfalz* (Rhineland-Palatinate) borders on France, Belgium and Luxemburg. Less perhaps than any of the post-war states that now comprise West Germany can it look back on a continuous history. It was put together artificially by the occupation powers from a conglomeration of territorial bits and pieces that, if not earlier a unit within any of the many 'Germanies,' were part of the Roman Empire. There is probably not a square foot of the two provinces, once known as 'Germania inferior' and 'Germania superior' and now forming Rhineland-Palatinate, that has not been trodden by Roman soldiers. The part of the present day state that flanks the middle reaches of the Moselle once formed part of the Roman province of Belgica. On the opposite bank of the river was the starting point of the 'limes' or frontier posts beyond which lay barbarian territories that were never conquered by Rome. It would be unfriendly, therefore, as well as untrue, to suggest that this part of West Germany, in which the wings of history beat almost audibly, lacked a tradition of its own that was in its very different way as clearly defined as that of Bavaria or Hamburg.

After the Rhineland had been incorporated into the Frankish kingdom, the old Roman centres of Trier (the oldest town in Germany, as it claims), Mainz, Speyer and Worms became focal points of ecclesiastical organisation, as noble cathedrals still testify. Until the dissolution of the Holy Roman Empire the bishops of Trier, Mainz and the Palatinate were among the electors of its emperors. The cathedral of Mainz dates back to Archbishop Willigis (978), and the town was the home of Johannes Gutenberg, the father of printing. The cathedral of Speyer contains the tombs of eight emperors of the Holy Roman Empire, including Salians and Stauffer, as well as the better-known and more numerous Habsburgs. Worms is the town of the Nibelung legends and was from 416 to 493 the capital of the kingdom of Burgundy. But for all this fame it is better known for its association with the Reformation. It was the town where Luther, in 1521, defied the Diet of the *Reich*.

The inhabitants of Rhineland-Palatinate are concerned today with other matters than the contribution of their predecessors to the history of Europe and the world. Included within its area is the most romantic and beautiful stretch of the Rhine, the enchanting valley of the Moselle and the attractive Eifel hill country, but these are not great sources of wealth. Starting off as a markedly agricultural area (wine, vegetables, fruit, hops, sugar beet, etc.), the state has over the years developed trade and light industry to the point where these provide 52 per cent of its gross product, almost exactly equal to the average for the country. Its agricultural output has sunk to 6 per cent which compares with 4 per cent for the country, but the figures indicate the trend clearly enough. The vast expansion of the chemical industry in Ludwigshafen, where the great BASF combine has its headquarters, has been largely responsible for changing the economic character of the state. But just as likely to catch the eye of the visitor, and far more attractive to it, are the vineyards which, even though the Rhineland is better known abroad as a wine-producing area, account for over 77 per cent of the total output of the country. The 'Wine Street'—a chain of wine-producing villages that runs alongside the Haardt hills—attracts many tourists, and the climate is so mild that almond trees bear fruit.

Although the Rhineland is mainly Catholic, the proportion for the Rhineland-Palatinate taken as a whole is 58 per cent Catholic and 41 per cent Protestant. The state government has always been led by the Christian Democrat party.

THE SAARLAND

It is somewhat ironic that the Saarland, which because of its coal and steel riches was so long fought over by France and Germany, should now have become one of the needier West German states. Since the coming of oil, natural gas and nuclear energy as sources of power, and since synthetic plastics became important materials, coal and steel are no longer what they were in any country as a basis of prosperity. But besides this problem, the Saarland has to cope today with the fact that, during the decisive period between the end of the First World War and 1935 (when, with cries of *'Heim ins Reich,'* it became German again), its communications and economy were orientated to France. The economic reunion of the area with West Germany proved in the event more difficult than the political one (see also Chapter I—Historical Landmarks), with the result that special arrangements were required.

Under the Saar Treaty, which came into force at the same time as the economic reunion with West Germany (6 July 1959), there was a customs-free exchange of goods amounting to £90 million=$250 million a year from France to the Saarland and rather less than half the amount in the reverse direction. This arrangement was later incorporated in the Common Market agreements. Saarland social and other policies had also to be re-orientated from France to West Germany, and the process was not easy. Social insurance in particular had taken a course in France that was different from that in West Germany, and this involved the Saarlanders in a difficult transition period.

But since then a spur of the autobahn has been built by the federal authorities which links the Saarland to the main West German network, and much more has been done to link the area, both in its communications and in its economy generally, with the country to which it now belongs, it appears, for ever. The Saarland government itself has promoted other industries besides the traditional ones of coal and steel, with the result that agricultural and almost every other kind of machinery is now produced there as well as coal and steel, precision and optical instruments, and chemical, rubber and synthetic products. But the Saarland also likes to think of itself as playing a special part in the development of the Common Market. Its Franco-German history, and its geographical situation at a point where the Benelux countries as well as France and Germany meet, give it unique opportunities as a link. The coal seams of the Saarland (to give only one example), which are no respecters of political boundaries, provide opportunities for the French and Saarland mine managers to meet at frequent intervals to discuss common problems. They settle them far more easily than their masters settle the political problems of Paris and Bonn.

At school in Bad Godesberg.

Munich University.

The Regions

The Saarland is mainly Catholic—77 per cent—and its government is led by the Christian Democrats. It is inevitably a receiver of aid under the states financial equalisation scheme.

BERLIN

Berlin since the Second World War has found itself in the unhappy position of being a miniature version of the world's biggest problem. It is divided into east and west as, on a larger scale, Germany itself is divided, and as Europe on a larger scale still and finally the world itself (except for the uncommitted countries) are also divided. Both East and West Germany claim Berlin as a capital, but, since neither side has physical possession of more than half the city, neither can enforce its claims. West Germany is in the weaker position (see also Chapters I and II), since Berlin is buried deep in Communist-controlled East Germany. West Berlin is not even a West German state in the full sense of the word, since in the last resort the writ of the allied commandants still runs there—as indeed, because of the ever-present Russian shadow over it, the West Berliners and West Germans alike all wish it to run.

Traffic control by television.

New roads and a new bridge in Cologne.

Wartime destruction in Berlin was such that, when hostilities finally ended on 2 May, 1945, the rubble amounted to one-sixth of the total in all other German towns together—and that was vast. More houses were destroyed in Berlin than Munich ever possessed. But, such was the mood of the Russians who occupied the city alone for two months, that 80 per cent of its remaining industrial capacity was dismantled and either destroyed or removed to Russia, where it was useless because it could not be geared to the Russian system. More than three million people were living among the ruins at scarcely above starvation level.

For these reasons alone Berlin was bound to present a special problem to the western powers when, in accordance with the London protocol of September 1944, they arrived to take over their respective sectors. But the disagreements which finally led to the year-long (1948-9) Russian blockade of the western part of the city, and to its defeat by the American-British airlift, delayed the economic recovery which in West Germany was already beginning.

West Berlin is still cut off from its natural hinterland in East Germany and from West Germany, so that, as its political position is precarious, so its economic position is uncertain. It is politically 'free' or western only because western troops are there to prevent the surrounding 'red sea' from rushing in, and it is economically viable only on the basis of aid from outside. American and West German aid enabled a magnificent network of roadways to be built inside West Berlin that, while ahead of the city's present traffic requirements (limited because of its isolation), provided much-needed employment. Aid of various kinds (subsidies, loans, etc.) still accounted in 1967 for well over 50 per cent of the city budget. Many of the bigger West German firms expanded their existing industrial capacity in the city (electrical, machinery, etc.), or started up there for the first time, either in response to tax concessions or in a conscious attempt to give the city economic and thus political support. The Hamburg newspaper magnate Axel Springer (see Chapter VIII) built a new £9 million printing and publishing block there, alongside the Communist dividing wall, as much in a spirit of political

The Regions 93

defiance as out of commercial consideration. Siemens, Bosch, Telefunken and others have big investments in the city.

But if it is true, as is often said, that the prosperity of West Berlin is only a façade compared with that of West Germany, the people who live there continue to face up to their difficult lot in life with fortitude and characteristic good humour. Their city is still much visited, not only by business people—West Berlin is, in spite of all, the country's biggest manufacturing centre—but by those who wish to see for themselves the permanent east-west confrontation, symbolised since 13 August 1961 by the Communist wall, and above all by straightforward tourists. These find splendid shopping boulevards, above all the famous *Kurfürstendamm*, and fine theatres, art galleries, museums, etc. West Berlin is also blessed with fine woods and lakes without which its people would surely have died of claustrophobia during the blockade and even since, as communications are still, except for the air routes, hampered by Communist controls. The West Berlin city government is traditionally left-wing, with the Social Democrat Party leading coalitions. In the present government their coalition partner is the small Free Democrat Party. The largest single religious group is the Catholics with 251,100. But a larger number still, 273,800, are registered as being 'without religion.' The rest are Protestant, Jewish, of 'other religions' or have given no indication of their religion at all.

4

How They Live

HOUSING

WARTIME bombing and shelling destroyed or rendered completely uninhabitable 2.3 million homes in what is now West Germany. This was 20 per cent of the total. Less than half of the remaining dwellings were undamaged. Since 1949, when effective rebuilding began, more than nine million dwellings have been constructed to provide accommodation for more than 25 million persons. By 1966 there were, for every 10,000 persons in West Germany, 101 new dwellings, compared with 41 in East Germany.

From 1950 to the beginning of 1966 a total of £18,750 million=$52,500 million was spent on house-building. Of this, about 26 per cent came from public funds, 48 per cent from the capital market, and the rest from those for whom the houses were built. Public funds were used to keep rents and interest rates low for large sections of the population. But the aim of the authorities in using public funds was not merely to relieve the housing shortage. Their policy was at the same time to encourage as many people as possible to own their own houses or other dwellings. Thus special aid was given to low-income groups who planned to build or buy their own property, and to families with several children, war disabled, and war widows with children. By 1966, 4.5 million homes had been built under these arrangements, and 2.5 million of all new homes were privately owned.

Need was so great in the early years that standards were not so high as they have since become. By 1966 76 per cent of all new dwellings had four or more rooms including the kitchen. West Germany was called upon to provide during these years not only for its own population but for the millions of expellees and refugees who had come in from the east (see Chapter I—Population). The rate of building was the fastest in the world. For some years, from 1953 onwards, a new dwelling was completed almost every minute, day and night. In 1960 10.5 dwellings per thousand inhabitants were completed, compared with 9.1 in Sweden, the next highest. The figure for the United States was 7.1 and for Britain 5.9.

A review of the present housing situation showed that, during the next twenty years and taking account of the need for demolition and replacement as well as for new construction, six million dwellings will be required. The sites for these, including provision for shops, roads, schools, etc., will cover some 470 square miles. The assumption is made in this calculation that the present proportion will be preserved, under which between 30 and 40 per cent of the population live in 'one-family' houses and the rest in apartment blocks. The last census (1961) showed that roughly 5.5 million households owned their own house, while over eleven million were main tenants of the houses or flats they occupied. Some 2.6 million were sub-tenants. The total number of households was 19.4 million.

The style of housing is as varied as the regions making up the country. In the rural areas of Bavaria and some of the smaller towns the picturesque Swiss châlet style is still popular. In the Rhineland the standard is set by the never attractive and (when dirty) quite hideous covering of rough cast. In Westphalia a pleasant red-brick style prevails in both domestic and farm buildings, and widely-constructed gables generally give admirable proportions. In the Lüneburg Heath area, farm buildings are still often thatched. In Schleswig-Holstein there is much whitewashed brick, which is as pleasing as the Westphalian red, while in parts of the country where slate is produced, such as the Eifel hills near Bonn, it is used to good effect. But in all parts of the country there is a strong tendency, especially in the towns, to go from the traditional to the modern. This means, in the main, straight-lined uniformity applied to ever larger blocks of up to thirty storeys. But such buildings can be both attractive and certainly impressive in their own way. A new group of buildings near the Bonn *Bundeshaus* (house of parliament) is a model of its kind. It houses the press, a foreign embassy, government offices, a restaurant etc., and is designed in open style round a large courtyard with fountains.

HEATING AND HOUSEHOLD EQUIPMENT

Domestic heating in post-war housing is still sometimes based on the old-style and often decorative German *Kachelofen* (glazed tile stove), though brown coal brickettes and other relatively clean fuels have replaced the earlier wood and coal. But in West Germany, as in most other industrialised countries, oil-fired central heating is rapidly taking over from all other systems. Old and originally coke-fired installations are converted, and new ones are based from the start on oil. *Fernheizung* (long-distance heating) is the system under which hot water is supplied over considerable distances for radiators and the tap. The heated water comes from a central works, which may be a power-station producing both electricity and *Fernheizung* or merely the latter. The English-style open fireplace was never popular in Germany, but is found in a few old houses. If used at all, it is mainly for its pleasing appearance and is usually supplemented by more efficient forms of heating. Cooking is by electricity or gas, though some coke-fired kitchen stoves are still found in the country, while kitchen equipment generally is increasingly electrical. Washing machines and dishwashers are found in millions of homes, together with electric irons, coffee grinders, fruit juice presses, vegetable mills, mixers and other such labour-saving gadgets.

SERVANTS

Domestic help in West Germany, as in most industrialised communities, is much harder to come by than in the past. When found at all, it is in the country rather than towns, though even there it can be had only by those able and willing to pay up to about 10s. (say $1.25) an hour. Demand is kept down, especially in the kitchen, by labour-saving devices, but the old-fashioned *Putzfrau* (charwoman who does cleaning by the day) is still much in demand in middle- and upper-middle-class households.

FOOD AND DRINK

The German is universally and quite rightly regarded as a *Wurst* (sausage) eater. The *Wurst* is made in dozens of regional varieties, most of which are found nowadays in all parts of the country. There is *Wurst* for frying (*Bratwurst*), and for heating in hot but not boiling water (*Bockwurst*). There are numerous varieties for eating as they are, though sliced (*Mettwurst, Katenwurst, Bierwurst, Schinkenwurst,* etc.), while others are for spreading on bread (*Teewurst, Leberwurst*). Some varieties of *Wurst* must be eaten fresh (e.g. the Munich *Weisswurst*—white sausage), while others will keep for years. The kitchen in Germany is otherwise based, in the matter of meat, first on pork and then on veal and beef. Germans eat little lamb and less mutton. Fish is eaten in relatively large quantities near the seaports, but the amount diminishes as distance from the sea increases. There is no *haute cuisine* in Germany, but many of the local dishes, especially the hearty, peasant ones of Bavaria, can be very good indeed—above all on a winter's day after a long walk. They include boiled knuckle of pork eaten with sauerkraut or pease pudding, and Kasseler—mildly smoked and cured pork eaten to the same accompaniment. Game is of excellent quality, and in general very well prepared. There are few better dishes in the season than saddle of venison or hare.

Germany is one of the few remaining industrial countries where bread-making is still highly regarded. Bread is available in some 200 varieties and is made of rye as well as wheat, and of mixtures of the two. It may be black, brown or white, according to the mixture, and a variety of intermediate shades. *Vollkornbrot* (wholemeal bread) is of a rich, dark colour and the perfect accompaniment to most kinds of *Wurst*. *Nachtisch*, or dessert, is indifferent. It is usually gelatin, or preserved fruit, or something of the sort. German cheese is undistinguished, but French cheese has, since the Common Market, become generally available. Salads are usually (not quite always) abominable, and fresh green vegetables hardly obtainable in restaurants.

The national alcoholic drink is beer, but West Germany produces some of the finest white wine in the world, and some indifferent red wine, and both are drunk widely. As well as from barley, beer is produced in small quantities, mainly in Bavaria, from wheat. Wine comes mainly from the Rhine and Moselle valleys, though also from Franconia and Baden. Schnaps (colourless spirits) are distilled from grain and fruit (cherries and raspberries). They may be drunk before or after a meal, though they should always be very cold. Mineral waters abound in Germany at the innumerable *Kurorte* (spas), and are highly esteemed, whether for medicinal purposes or as normal table waters.

Germans begin their gastronomic day with coffee (and tinned milk), a roll and butter and perhaps a boiled egg. This is *Frühstück* (breakfast) and is eaten early, since the working day starts generally at eight. But it is likely to be followed by a *zweites* (second) breakfast in the form of a *Wurst* or ham sandwich eaten at the office desk or factory bench. The midday meal, which tends to be the main one of the day, is eaten in office or works canteen. The canteen habit is the result of the realisation by employers that it saves much travelling time to and from outside restaurants. This point is of additional importance in the growing number of overcrowded areas, where offices as well as factories find it necessary to spread out beyond town centres. There are often no restaurants at all within reasonable distance. The evening meal at home may be anything from a simple plate of *kalter Aufschnitt* (cold cuts of *Wurst*, ham, etc.), with potato salad or bread or *Eintopf* (stew) or, among the more prosperous classes, a chop or steak.

HOW THEY SPEND THEIR MONEY

The West German people had plenty of money to spend when the war ended, but it was in the form of the paper *Reichsmark*, inflated to the point of worthlessness. For that matter there was nothing in the shops for them to spend money on. Their shopping was limited to what they could buy on the black market with the only acceptable currency—black market cigarettes bought at the price of six *Reichsmarks* each. But on 20 June 1948 came the currency reform and things changed overnight. The shops, if not full, were at least well stocked with goods that had been kept out of sight until life for private consumers—*Normalverbraucher* they were called—began again. But for a time the going was still hard since only 40 *Reichsmarks* could be exchanged for the new and valuable *Deutschemark* at the rate of one for one. All other paper *Reichsmarks* were declared non-legal tender and ordered to be delivered to the banks. The owners of bank accounts received only six-and-a-half of the new marks in exchange for a hundred of the old.

The standard of living was, in those early post-war years, so low that even with the aid of food brought in by Britain and America to their respective zones of occupation, it remained well below what nutrition experts regarded as a subsistence minimum. In terms of calories it stood at some 1,000 compared with 3,000 or more today. But private consumption as a whole in West Germany is still well below that of Britain and only a little more than half as high as in America.

A breakdown of the way money is spent by the *Normalverbraucher* shows that a much smaller proportion of his total income goes on food and clothing than in the early years. This is natural enough in any society where incomes continue to rise beyond the point where they cover basic material needs. But in West Germany this development has been reinforced by the fact that food and clothing prices have risen less than most: food by only 33 per cent since 1950 and clothing by 18 per cent. Yet from the year of the currency reform to its twentieth anniversary in 1968, money incomes rose by 450 per cent and real incomes (i.e. allowing for price increases) by 300 per cent.

The limit of satisfaction for that other basic necessity of the consumer, accommodation, was slower in being met, even at minimum standards. This was a consequence of the vast wartime destruction and the influx of refugees (see also this chapter—Housing). Thus if the three items rent, heating and house-furnishing are taken together, the expenditure has not fallen since 1950 but has risen from 23 to 26 per cent. This is, however, partly explained by the fact that rents have gone up by 79 per cent, which is far more than the average of all consumer price rises.

The greatest increase in consumer expenditure since 1950 has been on transport. Since here the price increase at 31 per cent was comparatively small, the increased expenditure (nearly five times as much) reflects a genuine growth in consumption. It is largely the consequence of the enormous spread of motoring. In 1950 there was only one car to every ninety-two inhabitants, while in 1965 one person in six had a car of his own. In 1952 there were in West Germany eighteen cars for every 1,000 inhabitants and 157 in 1965 (see also Chapter VII).

There has been an almost equal increase since 1950 in consumer expenditure on such items as watches and clocks, jewellery and insurance premiums. This no doubt reflects in part the growing prosperity of a society advancing towards 'welfare' status, but the nearly fivefold increase was also accompanied by an 84 per cent price rise, so that the quantity increase was lower. There was a nearly fourfold increase in the amount spent on education and entertainment and a price increase of 45 per cent.

The amount spent by a single household (of parents and two children of whom one is under fifteen) on consumer goods averaged in 1966 £79=$220 a month. Of this total 40 per cent went on food and drink, 12 per cent on clothing, 11 per cent on rent, 10 per cent on household goods, and the rest, in amounts under 10 per cent, on transport, cosmetics, education and entertainment. The average consumption of cigarettes among potential smokers was 2,114 a head and of beer (among persons over fifteen) 336 pints. All these figures showed a steady increase over previous years—e.g. the amount available to the family in 1963 was £64=$180 a month and this was 70 per cent more than ten years earlier (40 per cent after allowing for price rises).

But as well as on material goods, the West German people have spent money—with government encouragement—on 'people's shares' and other forms of saving. Such encouragement has indeed been at the heart of the social policy of every government since the war. The right-wing Christian Democrat party in particular holds strongly that property ownership by the small man can and does contribute in a most important way to the stability of society. It so happened that the vast industrial enterprises the post-war federal authorities inherited from their Nazi predecessors placed them in a particularly favourable position for the pursuit of this policy. Among these enterprises were the Volkswagen car works, which over the years have become the biggest in the world outside America, the Preussag coal and steel concern, and the VEBA mining and electrical undertaking. These were partially 'privatised,' that is to say large blocks of shares in them were sold to the public—with preferences and reduced prices for low-income groups. The success of the policy at first exceeded all expectations. Within a few days of the announcement some 216,000 persons applied for Preussag shares to the par value of £2.6 million=$7.1 million. Volkswagen came next; 1,547,000 persons applied for shares with a par value of £30.6 million=$85.7 million.

But for all the enthusiasm at the start the government would today probably not claim that its people's shares policy had been a complete success. The hope was that the people would not only buy the shares but keep them as a permanent form of property. But what happened in practice was that large numbers of the new shareholders sold out as soon as they could do so at a profit—and that was very soon, since the buying price for the small man had been artificially low. The fact appears to be that the traditional dislike of small German investors for shares of any kind—even people's shares sponsored by their own government—stood in the way of the government's hopes. However, although there are far fewer small investors in West Germany than in either Britain or America, the number tends to grow, as is shown by the great Bayer Chemical group, whose share capital of £133 million=$375 million is owned by about 245,000 shareholders, including 16,500 of the firm's staff.

More conventional ways in which the government promotes the accumulation of property are through the tax system and by offering special incentives. Income tax, for example, has been so readjusted over the years that the amount payable on small incomes has fallen by nearly 80 per cent. Since 1958 a 'splitting system' has been in force which eases the income tax burden on married couples and so enables them to save more. The income of husband and wife (and very many wives have incomes from their work in shops, offices, factories, etc.), are added together and then halved and taxed separately. This means less danger for either partner of getting into a higher tax group. The 1958 law also raised the amount of tax-free income from a basic £80 to £150=$225 to $420. A married couple with one child pay no tax until their joint income exceeds £43=$121 a month and, if they have three children, not until it reaches £69=$194.

But as well as creating the *possibility* of saving in these ways, the government seeks to encourage the positive *will* to save— e.g. by offering under the Saving Bonuses Act of 1959 a 20 per cent bonus, additional to normal interest, on money saved in a calendar year and left untouched for five years. Only limited amounts may be saved in this highly profitable way, though the limit is higher for older people and those with several children. Tax relief is also granted to those who save through the medium of life insurance. Perhaps with a view to overcoming the dislike of stocks and shares, the government also grants bonuses in certain cases on the initial acquisition of fixed-interest securities and investment certificates.

If on the one hand these various measures stemmed from the

basic social philosophy of the government, they were also inspired by practical economic sense. It must be remembered that, following wartime destruction and the wiping out of vast private savings, West Germany was very short indeed of capital. Then, because of their wartime loss of savings, the people were very unwilling to take the same risk again. They were, in short, very disinclined to save and spent their money as soon as they acquired it on—in the first phase—food and drink, on refurnishing and the like and then on cars, foreign travel, etc. But they are now taking advantage of these various schemes, which include also the encouragement of house building. The building societies administered in 1965 some six million building contracts to the value of £10,570 million=$29,600 million. This again (see Chapter II—Currency) showed confidence in the new *Deutschemark*. The insurance density (i.e. the number of life policies per 1,000 inhabitants) rose from 540 in 1952 to 838 in 1965. Small policies (up to £450=$1,250) accounted for nearly 59 per cent of the total. The total coverage within this group was just over 18 per cent of life insurance as a whole. At the other end of the scale the largest policies accounted for only 22 per cent of total policies, though for 64 per cent of the cover. These policies were mainly in the hands of self-employed persons in handicraft, trade and industry, and of professional persons for whom they represented a most valuable way of saving and establishing a degree of financial independence.

The gross earnings from which all expenditure and all savings were made rose in the case of male industrial workers from only just over £4=$11.5 a week in 1950 to £19=$52.75 in 1967. The comparable figures for Britain and America in 1967 were £20 and $100. But it must be remembered that figures in money are only a rough guide. Price rises in the three countries (and in all others) vary considerably, and so do the commodities and other items on which people in different countries spend their money. Earnings for women are also appreciably lower than for men. For example, while current (1968) salaries for male office clerks in industry and commerce are a little over £88=$246 a month, those for females are £56=$157.

SOCIAL SECURITY

The philosophy behind all West German legislation on social security is that, while the state should come to the aid of the individual in all cases where through no fault of his own—sickness, accident, old age—he is in need, his ultimate responsibility to himself should not be undermined. This means in practice that the individual is given no general claim on the state for his subsistence and no national health service on the British model is either in being or planned.

But within these limits the social security plans which started in 1881 are as old and extensive as any in the world. The state contributes a steadily rising figure that amounted in 1967 to 33.5 per cent of the total national budget. That is more than under any other head of national expenditure. The view is taken that the standard of living of the insured should not seriously deteriorate at times of sickness or unemployment. This (as will be seen below) is reflected in relatively high, and under some headings rising, contributions from employed and employer. But contributions can also fall—and have done in the case of unemployment insurance. And benefits are high; cash payments to the sick can reach 100 per cent of net earnings, and retirement pensions have doubled since 1957. Indeed in the case of pensions, not only is the principle applied that the *real* value must be maintained, that is to say the money pension must rise at the same rate as prices, but the pension must also be 'dynamic'—it should rise even faster than prices in order to allow the pensioner to share in the growing prosperity of the community.

While in Britain the national insurance Acts are applied to persons described collectively as employees, the distinction is still made in West Germany between *Arbeiter* (manual workers) and *Angestellte* (office staff). Thus *all Arbeiter* are compulsorily insured under all plans, but there is still a limit—of £80=$225 a month—above which sickness insurance is for *Angestellte* on a voluntary basis only, with the employer making no contribution. All limits under other insurance headings have been abolished (retirement pensions since 1968 only) but there are still, as will be seen, differences in benefits, and *Arbeiter* and *Angestellte* plans are administered through different organisations.

Contributions under the sickness insurance plan vary slightly, but averaged in 1968 about 10 per cent of the insured person's earnings. This amount is shared equally between the employee and the employer, with the state making no contribution except in the case of the special miners' fund, to which it pays 1 per cent of insurable earnings. The sickness insurance plan covers some 87 per cent of the population—twenty-nine million directly-insured employees and their twenty-one million wives and children.

Arbeiter throughout the country are members of their local general fund, which pays for the whole of their medical treatment at basic levels, including hospital treatment. More specialised treatment will not necessarily be covered in full, though it may be, and if the patient wishes to go into something other than the ordinary public ward at the hospital he will have to pay the difference. He must also make a payment of 2s.=25 cents towards the cost of medicines. Convalescence is also largely covered by the plan, and this may include a stay at one of the many West German spas. These are highly specialised in heart, circulation, lung and liver complaints etc., and are much more used than in, say, Britain or the US, where they have been out of fashion for two generations.

The sickness plan is administered in the case of *Angestellte* by semi-public corporations known somewhat curiously as substitute funds (*Ersatz Kassen*). The basic benefits are much the same as for the *Arbeiter*, except that the insured persons may have a somewhat wider choice of doctor. But the choice is limited for all to those doctors who are on the registered panel of the local general or the substitute funds.

Cash benefits for the sick *Arbeiter* are for the first six weeks at the rate of 65 per cent of earnings, plus allowances for family, though with 75 per cent as a maximum. In addition, employers are required to pay a supplement that brings the total up to 100 per cent of net earnings. After the first six weeks this supplement falls away, but benefits otherwise continue much as before. They are payable for a total of seventy-eight weeks within any three years. *Angestellte* receive full salary for the first six weeks, and thereafter the same rate of benefits as *Arbeiter*.

Some fifteen million persons a year receive medical benefits, 2.5 million of them in hospital. Total expenditure under the scheme in 1966 was £1,666 million=$4,625 million, including £471 million=$1,325 million for medical and dental treatment, £285 million=$800 million for hospital care and £356 million=$1,000 million in cash allowances.

Retirement or old age pensions are in general payable at sixty-five, but they are coupled with an 'invalidity' scheme, which means that women and those who have become partially or wholly incapacitated before retirement age have a claim. As with sickness insurance, contributions are related on a percentage basis to earnings. Benefits are calculated on the basis of the number of the years for which contributions have been paid. The rate of contributions rises in order that the real value of the pension may be maintained and so that the 'dynamic' principle may be applied. The rate of contribution, shared equally between employer and employee, was 15 per cent of the insured person's income in 1968, but an increase of 1 per cent per annum has

Autobahn across the Hasel valley in the Spessart.

Crossing the Rhine by overhead gondola at Cologne—believed to be the only one of its kind in the world.

been fixed up to 1971. There is, however, a maximum contribution fixed for each year, which means that those whose contribution on a percentage basis would have been above it do not pay on the part of their income that would have brought their contribution above the maximum. The maximum for 1968 was £18.36=$60 a month, and it will rise by 1971 to £29=$81. Since pensions are related both to earnings and years of service, it is not easy to state just how much they are, but a typical case based on roughly average earnings in 1968 (£73=$200 a month) and forty years' service would be about £38=$107 a month—rather more than 50 per cent of earnings.

The number of *Arbeiter* covered by the pensions plan is 16,500,000, and of those actually drawing pensions about 3,700,000. The figures for *Angestellte* were in 1967 about 8,500,000 persons covered, either compulsorily or voluntarily, and 2,200,000 receiving pensions. But with the abolition of the income limit for *Angestellte* in 1968 the number of insured rose by about 125,000. This was only about half as many as it might have been, since many of the newcomers chose to take advantage of a clause which enabled them to provide their own cover on the commercial insurance market, so long as it was not less than it would have been under the state scheme.

Old wine house at Bacharach on the Rhine.

Dinkelsbühl in Bavaria.

There is a sociological trend away from the *Arbeiter* and towards the *Angestellte* occupations. This means that, as *Arbeiter* reach retirement age and begin to draw their pensions, the contributions they have been paying into the *Arbeiter* Pension Fund will not be fully made good by a new generation. Many of the potential *Arbeiter* will, in short, become *Angestellte* instead. Thus, in mid-1968, figures were published which showed a deficit in the *Arbeiter* Fund and a surplus in the *Angestellte* Fund. But as the surplus on the one by no means covered the deficit on the other, there will be by 1972 a net deficit of £1,080 million=$3,000 million. The contributions of the *Angestellte* newly-brought into the plan will help, but other measures not yet decided upon will be needed.

All *Arbeiter* and *Angestellte* are covered, since the income limit for *Angestellte* was abolished in 1967, by unemployment insurance. But because unemployment in West Germany has, since the economic recovery of the fifties, been in general low, though it rose a little during the recession of 1966-7, it has been possible to reduce the rate of contribution, shared equally by employed and employer, from 2 to 1.3 per cent. There is no contribution from the state, which does, however, bear the full cost of unemployment assistance in cases where entitlement to insurance benefit has run out.

Cash benefits are on a graduated scale, payable after three waiting days, in proportion to average earnings over the previous thirteen weeks. There is also a supplement for each dependant, adult or child. Benefits can rise to 75 per cent in the case of low previous earnings, but may be around 30 per cent for higher ones. Unemployment assistance rates—subject to a means test—are slightly lower than the insurance benefits, but under both schemes help is given where necessary in retraining for alternative employment.

Accident insurance is paid by the employer only, who contributes to an industrial injury insurance society. The rate varies widely, since the risk of injury is very different as between one occupation (e.g. mining) and another (e.g. clerk). The average paid by employers is about 1.4 per cent of their wages bill, though in mining it is 14 per cent. The plan covers journeys between home and work as well as in the factory, office, etc., retraining and rehabilitation, artificial limbs, daily cash allowances and pensions.

Industrial injury benefit is payable from the day of the accident, and if it is clear after thirteen weeks that there has been a permanent loss of earning capacity of 20 per cent or more, then the question of a pension arises. For total incapacity, benefit is two-thirds of earnings and for partial loss (over 20 per cent) at a proportional rate. Widows' pensions up to 30 per cent of the late husband's earnings are payable up to remarriage—otherwise for life. On remarriage the widow receives a lump sum equal to five years' pension. Orphans' pensions are also payable up to the age of eighteen. All benefits are adjusted from time to time in accordance with the cost of living.

Since industrial or other wages and salaries take no account of the number of children of the employed, the state has provided a plan to which it alone contributes. Since 1964 all families with three or more children have received allowances. The amounts are £4 9s. 3d.=$12.50 a month for the third child, £5 7s. 2d.= $15.00 for the fourth and £6 5s. 0d.=$17.50 for the fifth and all subsequent ones. An allowance is paid for the second child only if the parents' income falls below £54=$150 a month. Payment is normally made up to the age of eighteen, but may be continued to twenty-five if the young person is still receiving education, training, etc., at the parents' expense.

HEALTH SERVICES

Largely as a result of the growth and improvement in the health services in West Germany, as in other advanced countries, such former scourges as tuberculosis have been in the main overcome, but other causes of death have taken their place. Thus, although only thirteen persons in every 100,000 died of tuberculosis in 1964, heart and circulation disorders accounted for 42 per cent of all deaths. Cancer was the cause of over 19 per cent. But thanks to compulsory vaccination (soon after birth and at the age of twelve) smallpox has been mastered, while voluntary vaccination has helped greatly in combating scarlet fever, diphtheria and whooping cough.

There are 504 public health offices, whose task is to reduce or eliminate the danger of epidemics and to supervise the use of medical preparations, poisons, narcotics, etc. They also concern themselves with food hygiene, and keep a watch on medical staff. There is a pharmacy to every 5,981 inhabitants and about 60 per cent of the 84,200 doctors have their own practices. Of this total 14,599 are women, and there are 2,599 auxiliary medical practitioners. There are 159,114 persons tending the sick in hospitals, etc., including 109,797 nurses, trained or under training. In addition there are 13,427 children's nurses and 32,047 dentists.

More than half the hospitals in the country are maintained by the public authorities (federal, state or municipal) and the national insurance societies, and more than one-third by the churches and voluntary welfare organisations. There are 106 hospital beds available for every 10,000 inhabitants and the average time spent in hospital by every patient is twenty-eight days.

5

How They Work

INDUSTRY

IN 1875 only forty persons in every 1,000 were employed in industry, but by 1965 the figure was 143. In that year also 8.46 million persons were in industry. There were at the same time 103,700 industrial enterprises, of which 1.2 per cent employed 1,000 or more, while 6.2 per cent employed 200 to 999 and 48.9 per cent from 10 to 199. Most industrial employees (81 per cent) work in enterprises with more than 100 on the staff. A process of expansion in the size of industrial units is going on, though the pace is not so fast as in Britain and America. It is limited mainly to basic industrial processes, and by changes in the tax system and in company law the government is seeking to check the trend.

The main emphasis in industrial production is on manufacturing, which accounts for about 87 per cent of the whole. Of this, basic materials account for 29 per cent, capital goods for 31 per cent, consumer goods for 16 per cent and food for 11 per cent. In the non-manufacturing sector, mining accounts for 5 per cent, power for 5 per cent and building for 4 per cent.

The rate of expansion in 1965 was greatest in the consumer goods industry—9.5 per cent. Earlier it had been the capital goods industry, with 12 per cent in 1961 but 9.1 per cent in 1965. The average increase from 1964-5 was 8 per cent.

West German recovery from wartime destruction, which became world-famous as the 'economic miracle,' was made possible by the currency reform of 20 June 1948, which put an end to inflation, and by the great American Marshall Plan programme of aid. The process gathered impetus in the fifties so that the gross national product, the total of all goods and services produced and provided, grew far more rapidly than in countries, including Britain and America, that had little or no such recovery to make. Thus it increased more than fourfold (432 per cent) from 1950 to 1965, when it stood at £40,070 million=$112,200 million. During the first phase (to 1955) this was an average annual rate of growth of 9.4 per cent as compared with 2.7 per cent in Britain and 4.3 per cent in the United States. In the second phase (to 1960) the rate had declined somewhat to 6.3 per cent, compared with 2.2 per cent in Britain and the same in the United States. In the next phase (to 1965) something like normal conditions had been reached, and the rate of growth was 4.3 per cent, compared with a slightly increased 2.7 per cent in Britain and a distinctly higher 4.6 per cent in the United States. The policy of the government in 1968 was to keep the economy 'steady as she goes' with an annual rate of growth into the seventies of about 4 per cent. It is believed that this rate will avoid the 'overheating' which led to the recession of 1966-7, and yet permit full or nearly full employment to be restored and maintained. Thus the gross national product figure for 1967 rose only modestly from the 1965 level to about £43,000 million=$121,000 million. Of this total the manufacturing industries contributed 41 per cent and industry as a whole, including mining, power supplies etc., 57 per cent. Trade, transport and communications accounted for 23 per cent, and agriculture etc. for the rest.

COAL

Though not lavishly blessed with natural resources, West Germany has large supplies of coal. The largest deposits are in the Ruhr, and they are estimated at 65,000 million tons, which at the present rate of consumption (which is, however, declining) should last 500 years. There are also some 5,000 million tons of brown coal (lignite) deposits in West Germany, which should

How They Work

last fifty years. Coal has traditionally been the chief source of power, but it is being steadily replaced by oil. From 1963 onwards pits were being closed every year, and the output of coal reduced, though not quite correspondingly, since improved production methods increased the man-shift output in mines that remained in operation. In 1963, 142 million tons were mined and in 1965 135 million. Under present planning, output will, by 1970, be down to about 90 million tons a year. The total cost of closing pits, re-training miners etc., had by the middle of 1967 reached some £30 million=$79 million, of which half was borne by the state. But the steady decline of the industry is a national problem that has not yet been solved. In the Ruhr area itself it has led to serious unrest, culminating at times in large-scale demonstrations by miners who have lost their jobs or are threatened by loss of them. In 1950 coal accounted for 90 per cent of the total primary power supply in West Germany, but by 1965 the figure was down to 54 per cent. Over the same period oil rose from 5 to 41 per cent. By 1966 the share going to coal was down to 38 per cent and the trend was continuing. In 1967 oil accounted for 46 per cent of the total and thus replaced coal as the chief source of primary power. Of 387,746 miners, 224,539 work underground.

OIL

Oil wells in north Germany produce seven to eight million tons a year. But as this figure remains almost constant and total consumption grows, the percentage of home-produced to imported oil falls. It was 17 per cent in 1962, but only slightly more than 10 per cent in 1967. Total consumption rose by nearly 4 per cent in 1967 to 81 million tons.

GAS

As the coal industry contracts, it becomes decreasingly important as the source of gas. Its place is being taken by natural gas, of which West German production rose sixfold between 1960 and 1967, to reach a total of more than 300,000 million cubic yards. More was imported from Holland, and, as new sources are discovered in both West Germany and Holland, consumption is expected to rise.

ELECTRICITY

The total volume of electricity generated in West Germany rose from 172,000 million kilowatt-hours in 1965 to 192,000 million in 1967. Of the total, some 60 per cent was used by industry and 13 per cent by domestic households. The rest was used by trade, commerce, transport, agriculture and public facilities.

ATOM POWER

Atomic energy as a source of power for commercial purposes is in West Germany, as in other industrial countries, of relatively slight present importance but of immense potential significance. It accounts at present for 0.8 per cent only of all electrical power, but when new plant now under construction comes into operation in 1972 the figure will rise to 4 per cent.

OTHER MINERAL RESOURCES

West Germany imports most of its iron ore requirements from Sweden (a small quantity also from France), but it has some deposits of its own. They amount to about 3,000 million tons and are located in the foothills of the Harz mountains. As the quality of the ore is not high, production tends to fall. In 1965 it reached nearly eleven million tons (35 per cent of total requirements), but by 1967 had fallen to under eight million tons.

Pre-war Germany produced 96 per cent of the world's output of potash salts which are vital for agriculture, but a large part of the total of 2,000 million tons are in what is now East Germany. The West German production of 22 million tons in 1965 was one quarter of world output.

IRON AND STEEL

In 1965 West German blast furnaces smelted 33.5 million tons of imported iron ore and 7.5 million tons from home mines. The figure of 36.8 million tons of steel produced was the highest (42.8 per cent) among the countries of the European Coal and Steel Community. It compared with 27.4 million tons in Britain and 121.9 million tons in the United States. West German production in 1968 is expected to be 38 million tons. The number of employees in the iron and steel industry is about 350,000. Turnover is about £2,822 million=$7,900 million.

MOTOR VEHICLES

The motor vehicle industry runs neck and neck with that of Japan, which means second in the world after the United States. The industry thus takes its place among the three or four most important in the country, and its fortunes reflect the state of the entire economy. It led the 'economic miracle' of the fifties and early sixties, and declined in 1967 as a general economic recession set in. Total production of all vehicles, private and commercial, rose from 2,976,477 in 1965 to 3,050,708 in the following year, but fell in 1967 to 2,482,319. Throughout the early part of 1968 there was a general improvement, and the outlook for the rest of the year was one of cautious optimism. The industry has exported some 50 per cent of its output, but in the recession year of 1967 the figure rose to 59 per cent. This rise not only helped the industry itself to hold up against the fall in demand on the home market, but was of great value to the economy as a whole. As will be seen later in this chapter, industrial exports played a vital part in enabling the country to emerge in 1968 from the recession.

Of the ten car producers, Volkswagen is biggest by a long way. Its success story under Professor Nordhoff, who was appointed by the British at the end of the war and who died in April 1968, became symbolic of the whole post-war recovery. Starting in 1948, Professor Nordhoff raised production from 8,622 vehicles to 1,650,000 in 1966. This figure fell in the recession year of 1967 to 1,337,000, but showed signs in 1968 of picking up again. Most (70 per cent) of the production was of the famous 'beetle' model, of which more have been built than of any other single car model ever designed, excepting only Henry Ford's Tin Lizzie, of which 15,000,000 were made in eighteen years. But the 'beetle' is still in production at the rate of nearly a million a year, and in December 1965 the total of 10,000,000 was reached. Volkswagen are produced or assembled in Brazil, South Africa, Australia and Mexico, as well as in their home country. Chief importers are America where over 60 per cent of all imported cars are Volkswagens, followed by Holland, Belgium and Sweden. Volkswagen accounted in 1965 for 48 per cent of all West German motor vehicle production and 55 per cent of all exports. Its turnover of nearly £890 million=$2,500 million made it the biggest commercial undertaking in the country. Founded by the Nazis, it survived the war as a state-owned concern, but is now divided between the state and private shareholders.

Mercedes is West Germany's chief prestige car, while Opel (General Motors) and Ford are American-owned.

World production of motor vehicles in 1965 was 24,184,000 of which 9,335,200 were built in the United States and 1,722,000 in Britain. West Germany, as already stated, built 2,976,477. The motor vehicle industry employs about 520,000 persons.

ELECTRO-TECHNICAL

Siemens and Bosch are two great German names that spring at once to mind when the electrical industry is mentioned. They were among the pioneers, and the enterprises that they and their successors built up are among the most famous in the world. But others, including AEG (*Allgemeine Elektrizitäts-Gesellschaft*) and Telefunken and Brown Boveri (partly Swiss) are now in the same class. These firms and others make a vast range of equipment, varying from kitchen appliances (electric refrigerators, washing machines, dishwashers, electric irons, etc.), to radio and television sets and every kind of electrical equipment for industry—generating and distributing plant, telecommunication gear and specialised laboratory and electronic equipment. Siemens won in early 1968 the first great West German export contract for atomic power plant. Total production of the industry was slightly lower in 1966 than in 1965 (£2,822 million=$7,900 million), and a little lower again (5.3 per cent) in 1967 compared with the previous year. But the electro-technical industry, like so many others, compensated for the fall of demand during the period of recession in 1966-7 by increasing its exports by 9.5 per cent. The industry's normal export quota is about 19 per cent. Of its total production, rather more than two-thirds is investment and the rest consumer goods. The number of people employed in the industry fell by 7.6 per cent between 1966 and 1967, when the total was 874,593. The business outlook for 1968, for the electro-technical as for most industries, was much improved.

CHEMICALS

The West German chemical industry shares roughly with Britain second place in the world after America. Its three biggest firms—Bayer, Hoechst and BASF (*Badische Anilin und Soda*

Fabrik) are the parts into which the great pre-war IG Farben was broken down by the allies under the occupation policy of deconcentrating industry. Germans have always been leaders in the chemical and pharmaceutical field, and Bayer alone, although smaller than Britain's ICI, is the biggest chemical concern on the European mainland. There is a tendency towards reconcentration in the industry, and the firms named have all been engaged recently in something of a battle to absorb smaller units. The production programme of the industry ranges from dyes and fertilisers to oils, fats and cosmetics; from paint and printing ink to explosives and fireworks; and from synthetic resins and plastics to aspirin, saccharin (first produced by German chemists) and every kind of drug, including 'the pill.'

Turnover more than doubled during the ten years ending in 1965, when it reached £3,021 million=$8,434 million. It has been rising steadily ever since, and was less affected than most by the recession of 1967. The number of employed in the industry was 538,000 in 1966 and its export quota was 25 per cent.

ENGINEERING AND MACHINERY

The field covered by this heading is vast, and includes Krupp of Essen, Demag (*Deutsche Maschinenbau Aktiengesellschaft*), Klöckner-Humbolt-Deutz of Duisburg and Cologne respectively, and scores and indeed hundreds of others. Together with the motor vehicle, electro-technical and chemical industries, they carry the main weight of the West German economy. Only the consumer goods industries, in their wide variety, are comparable. Krupp, traditionally a personally-owned concern, became after the death in 1967 of Herr Alfried Krupp, a limited liability company. It produces everything from locomotives to orchids and false teeth (which do not perhaps quite come under the heading of either engineering or machinery), while Demag produces cranes, road construction machinery and the like, and

KHD, as it is more usually called, largely farm tractors. The industry is spread widely across the Ruhr and in the Frankfurt area, and to an increasing extent in Bavaria, where the firms MAN (Munich, Augsburg, Nürnberg) and Krauss-Maffei are dominant. MAN is closely associated in aircraft engine production with Rolls-Royce of Britain. The industry employs some 1,084,000 persons and had in 1965 a turnover of £3,443 million=$9,641 million. Its export quota is about 30 per cent.

SHIPBUILDING

In West Germany, as elsewhere in the world, the shipbuilding industry is something of a problem child. State aid in most of the big shipbuilding countries has, in the view of the Bonn government, so distorted the normal rules of competition that no shipyard knows quite how to plan. There has been some improvement, the government claims, since it took international action aimed at restoring normal conditions, but problems remain. In 1964 world output, with 2,032 new ships totalling 9.72 million tons, reached a new record. West Germany with 0.83 million tons, took third place after Japan and Sweden, and Britain, with 0.81 million tons, came fourth. There was public discussion in 1968 as to whether the two biggest West German shipyards, the largely state-owned Howald group and Blohm & Voss, should be merged in order to be able to meet Japanese competition more successfully, but no final decisions were taken. The shipping industry received a great boost in 1967, when a former Danish schoolmaster came to Hamburg and acquired the former Israeli liner *Shalom*. It had been unsuccessful under the Israelis (in part, apparently, because of the kosher cuisine), but under its new owner it took on a new lease of life as a luxury cruise ship. He named it after the earlier West German liner *Hanseatic*, which had been burnt out in New York harbour, and financed it largely with the aid of former passengers of the lost vessel. Its success was such that he was soon able to commission a second ship, the *Hamburg*. The two liners together have given West German shipping fresh prestige in world shipping.

West German shipyards work largely (44 per cent) for foreign account and employ 81,000 workers.

AIRCRAFT

One of the many consequences for Germany of defeat in the Second World War was that the development and expansion of its aircraft industry came, on allied orders, to an abrupt halt. The long break meant that, when the changing political scene and the reviving economy made it possible to start again, the industry was both technically and financially hopelessly backward as compared with America, Britain and France, where progress had been uninterrupted. When the military Luftwaffe and the civil Lufthansa came into being again in the middle fifties, they were both dependent on planes bought from America and, to a much lesser extent, Britain. They still are both very dependent, but the time has come when the infant new industry is insisting on the right to make at least some contribution to the country's aircraft requirements. It cannot for decades, if indeed ever, expect to do more than this, since the investment required for the design and development of modern aircraft whether military or civil, far exceeds the resources of West Germany. The industry's hope and aim, therefore, is that with the support of the Bonn government it will be able to play a worthwhile part in such joint projects as the civil 'airbus' (see also Chapter VII), in which France is also involved, and in the new European 'fighter of the seventies' plane on which talks in late 1968 were making good progress.

Some of the names that were familiar to the war generation—Messerschmitt, Dornier and Heinkel—are still current in the restarted industry, but others have come in. Among them is Bölkow, a small but growing south German firm that has conducted much secret research and development on helicopters and vertical take-off planes, and on rocket missiles on behalf of the government. The total number of companies engaged in air research and development is, at over forty, relatively large, but the trend to mergers is as compulsive in West Germany as in Britain and elsewhere. By a variety of complicated interlocking arrangements most of them are members of one of the three groupings known as Northern Group, Southern Group (1) and Southern Group (2). These main groupings include within themselves such smaller ones as the Bölkow and Dornier Groups, etc.

The total number of persons employed in the air and space industry in 1967 was about 45,000, while the turnover of the major companies was about £89 million=$250 million.

HANDICRAFT

For centuries craftsmen working with their hands and simple tools were the sole creators of both commercial goods and works of art. Noble cathedrals, fine sculptures and much else still testify to their skill. With the coming of the industrial revolution, craftsmen were superseded in many fields by mechanical processes but in others, including some of recent development (e.g. radio and television repairs), they remain indispensable. Their total number in 1965 was 3.7 million, or more than 44 per cent of all those in industrial employment. Their total was £11,936 million=$33,500 million. At the head of the list stood civil engineering with 786,100 persons employed and a turnover of £1,620 million=$4,525 million. Bakery and confectionery came second after a long gap in the numbers employed (253,800) though fourth in turnover with £820 million=$2,300 million. Butchery with 199,500 persons was sixth in numbers employed, but with £1,290 million=$3,600 million turnover second in turnover. Handicrafts as a whole contributed 11 per cent to the gross domestic product in 1965.

Handicrafts are regarded nationally as having great educational value. The old system of apprentices being trained to become first journeymen and then masters still prevails. In 1965 some 453,000 apprentices were being trained by masters in their workshops, and that number substantially exceeded the figure of those under training for industry. Every year more than 40,000 craftsmen pass their master's examination and are thus entitled to set up their own establishments.

AGRICULTURE

Germany began in the nineteenth century, in the wake of Britain, to turn from agriculture to industry and from the land to the towns. The process continued until the country became one of the most highly industrialised in the world. But no country likes to become entirely industrialised, to be entirely dependent—above all in time of war—on imported foodstuffs, or to lose a healthy balance between town and country life. Life in big towns and cities may be more stimulating, but life in the country still retains an innate desirability of its own. The dream of town folk is still for 'a cottage in the country.'

For such reasons as these the West German authorities have made immense efforts to make good the dislocation caused by the dismemberment of pre-war Germany. The part of the country

Gymnastics in West Berlin.

The international film festival in West Berlin; in the background are the war-damaged Memorial church and its postwar successor.

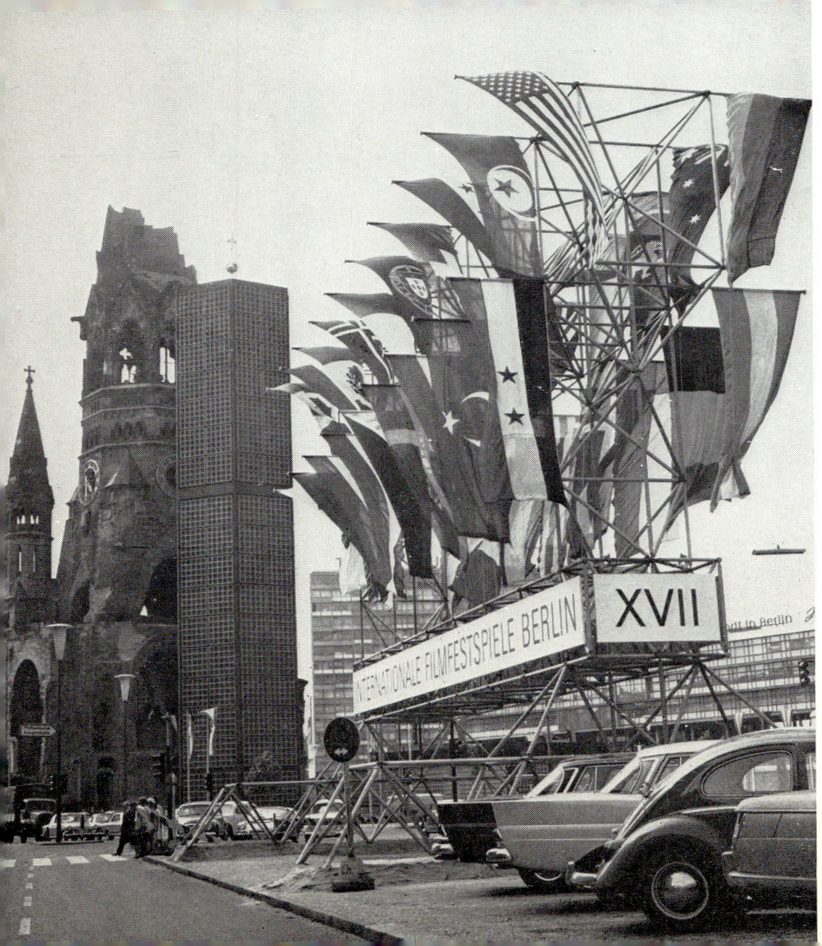
XVII
INTERNATIONALE FILMFESTSPIELE BERLIN

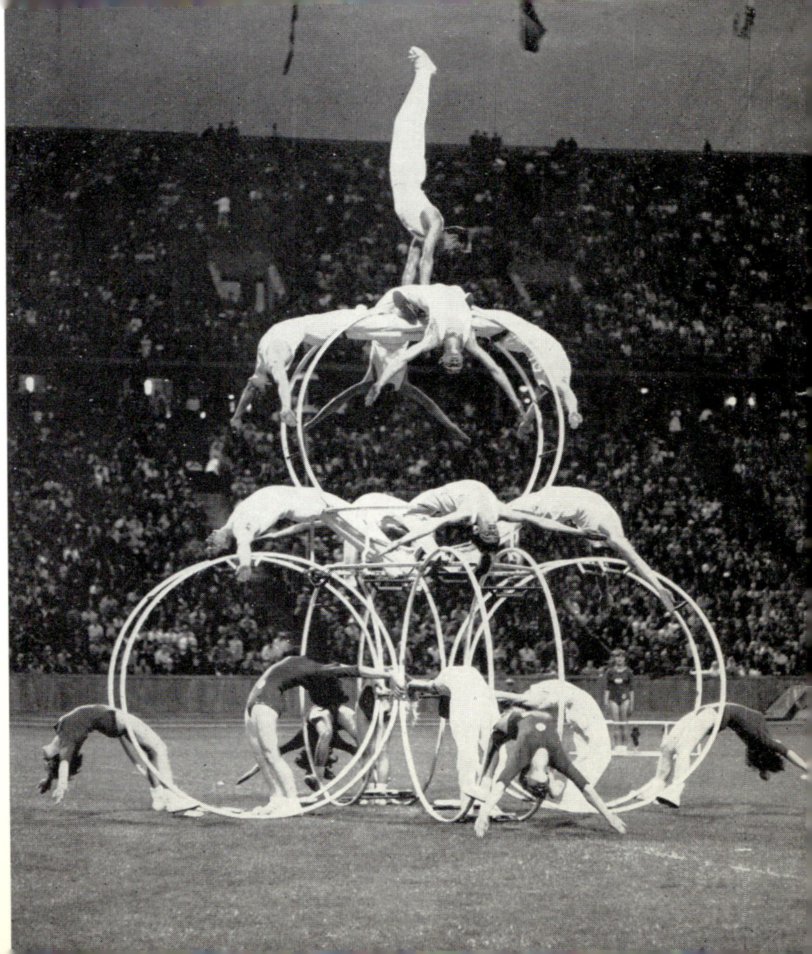

that has now become West Germany was—because it contained the Ruhr—largely industrial, while the eastern provinces produced 55 per cent of the grain, 57 per cent of the potatoes, and 66 per cent of the sugar beet consumed in the country as a whole. In the small and medium-sized holdings that predominate, the radical readjustment needed was far harder to bring about than in the big farms. Nevertheless *Flurbereinigung*, as the process of re-allocating the traditional 'strip' farms into rational and viable units is called, and scientific methods and fertilisers and machinery, have made it possible for West German farms to produce 75 per cent of the total grain needed by the country, 85 per cent of the bread grain, 86 per cent of the meat, and 52 per cent of the edible fats. Total food production is 162 per cent above the pre-war average, and only about a quarter of all foodstuffs consumed are imported. Most of the imports (nearly a quarter) are of the kind (tea, coffee, sub-tropical fruit, etc.) that cannot be produced in Germany. Agriculture has declined steadily from 10 per cent to a present 4 per cent of the gross national product, but since this itself has greatly increased, it does not mean an absolute decline in agricultural output. On the contrary, yields per acre have risen by a quarter and total production has doubled. Some 86 per cent of the total land

---

Carnival time in Baden-Württemberg.

Carnival time in the Rhineland.

area is used for agriculture and forestry, but since two-thirds of it is mountainous or hilly it is impossible for any kind of rationalisation or mechanisation to lead to large farms of the kind familiar in America. The total farming area is 32.6 million acres, and the average size of the 1.7 million farms (not including 5.5 million plots of an acre or less) is only 22 acres. But as the farming population has declined from 24 per cent of the total in 1950 to less than 10 per cent now, including families, manpower has been replaced by machinery. The number of combine harvesters has risen since 1950 from 1,000 to 120,000, of milking machines from 16,300 to 440,000, and of tractors from 90,000 to 1,137,000.

Of the total agricultural land, 54 per cent is arable, 41 per cent meadow and grazing land, and the rest is used for orchards, vineyards, etc. Of the arable land, 64 per cent produces grain, 20 per cent root crops, and the rest vegetables, forage, etc.

German inheritance laws vary widely—though especially as between north and south. In the north the firstborn is the heir, as is customary in Britain. The result is that the farms tend to be larger and more viable than those in the south, where there is division of the inheritance between the children. It is thus mainly in the south that a vast programme of re-parcelling of land has been undertaken by the government in a succession of 'Green Plans.' The aim has been to get rid of the unviable strip farms and replace them by larger and more coherent units. The smallest farm that will provide a family with a living is fifteen to thirty acres, according to location and manner of cultivation.

German farming is still much less highly-mechanised than in either Britain or America but the money spent on machinery in 1950 (£62 million=$173 million) had risen by 1965 to £255 million=$715 million.

Food production rose by 60 per cent during this period, in spite of the steady drain of farm-workers to the towns. The 1950 figure of twenty-nine whole-time workers for every 247 acres had fallen by 1965 to seventeen. Though behind Britain and America, West Germany is ahead of its Common Market partners in mechanisation. Expenditure so far in making these technical advances has been £3,570 million=$10,000 million, and under the green plans, grants and credits amount to £220 million=$625 million. Proceeds from the sale of agricultural produce in 1964-5 were £2,290 million=$6,425 million. Operational costs were £1,705 million or $4,775 million.

FISHERIES

Deep-sea and inshore fishery is in the hands of 1,677 concerns employing over 11,000 persons. In 1965 about 564,400 tons of fish, including shell-fish, were landed, of which 108,000 tons were herrings. The most important fishing-ground is the North Sea, which produces about one-third of the total catch. To meet total fish consumption per head (about 24 lbs.) some 270,000 tons of fish and fish preserves are imported annually.

FORESTRY

More than a quarter of West German territory is under timber, of which two-thirds are conifers. About 60 per cent of the total belongs to the state (federal or local authorities) and the rest is private. Between 1949 and 1964 about 321,230 acres of waste land were afforested. The forest land is managed by a total of 500,000 undertakings though of these, 1,900 manage more than half.

TRADE

Wholesale trade, brokerage and retail trade accounted in 1965 for 13.5 per cent of the West German total domestic product at current prices, or in absolute figures £30,270=$84,750. There is a slight tendency towards supermarket stores, but small businesses remain characteristic. Of these, almost 50 per cent had a turnover of less than £8,930=$25,000. More than a further 47 per cent had a turnover under £89,300=$250,000, leaving less than 3 per cent with a turnover above that figure. But these few accounted for 47 per cent of total turnover. The number of concerns in this class is increasing.

More than a third of all persons engaged in trade either own their own business or are dependants of the owners. The family business is thus characteristic, especially in retail trade. More than 50 per cent of all persons in trade are women—in retail trade 62 per cent. Of the total 439,000 retail establishments nearly half sell foodstuffs.

TRADE UNIONS AND EMPLOYERS' ASSOCIATIONS

Of the total of more than twenty-one million employees in West Germany, over eight million are members of trade unions. More than six and a half million of this number are in workers' or industrial unions that are affiliated to the German Federation of Trade Unions (*Deutscher Gewerkschaftsbund—DGB*) which is the equivalent of the British Trade Union Congress and the American Federation of Labour and Congress of Industrial Organisations. The rest belong to the German Office Staffs Union (*Deutsche Angestellten Gewerkschaft—DAG*) or the German Civil Servants' Union (*Deutscher Beamtenbund—DBB*).

West German industrial unions are so called because—like the American unions in the CIO, but unlike the British craft unions—they embrace all workers in any given industry, e.g. the Metal Workers Union, the Building Trades Union, etc. There are only sixteen of them in all compared with the 350 unions affiliated directly or indirectly to the British TUC. One important result of this is that negotiations between workers and employers are simplified. While in Britain employers may be required to make wage agreements with dozens or even scores of unions operating within any given industry, German employers (through their own organisations—see below) rarely have to deal with more than two unions—one industrial and the DAG.

The trade union structure is one of several factors that have contributed to labour-management relations which, while by no means free of disputes, are much more satisfactory than in Britain. A second factor is that since, with only one union to each industry, there are no 'demarcations' of the British kind, therefore no demarcation strikes. Thirdly, German law states that a strike is illegal unless a ballot of union members has been held in advance and 75 per cent have voted in favour. Thus the 'wild-cat' or unofficial strikes that account for most of the time lost in Britain are almost unknown in West Germany. While the average number of working days a year lost by strike action in Britain is about 2,500,000, that figure has never been reached in West Germany. The nearest approach was 2,320,927 days in 1957, but this was a great exception.

The figure is usually well below 100,000 (e.g. 16,700 in 1964; 48,500 in 1965 and 27,100 in 1966), but it rose in 1967 to 400,000. This compared with 2,764,000 in Britain. The figure for America for 1966 (1967 not available) was 25,165,000, though because of the much larger labour force this permits of no direct comparison. There are over 13 million members of the combined American AFL and CIO.

The West German trade unions are closely involved in the process of *Mitbestimmung*, or 'co-determination' as it is usually called in English. This means in practice that the workers—either directly through their works councils or indirectly through their representatives on supervisory and management boards—have a voice in the running of the undertakings in which they are employed. Co-determination is probably unique to West Germany, and derives from a series of three Acts passed under the influence of the occupying powers in the years between 1952 and 1956. It was never welcomed by employers but has come to be accepted by them, at least in its present form, and has undoubtedly played an important part in maintaining industrial peace.

In its first stage, co-determination means that the workers elect works councils who consult with the employers on a wide variety of matters affecting both sides—for example, social and welfare matters, safety measures in the factory, holidays, etc. But the works councils have no voice in the decisions of strict management, such as rationalisation and automatisation.

Secondly, the workers elect one-third of the members of the supervisory board. This organ has no parallel in Britain or America, where its functions are included in those of the board of directors. These functions consist of general supervision of the finances of the concern, whose day-to-day running, however, is in the hands of the *Vorstand* or board of management. The remaining two-thirds of the supervisory board (*Aufsichtsrat*) are chosen by the shareholders, and the *Aufsichtsrat* appoints the *Vorstand*.

Co-determination is taken a stage further in the coal, iron and steel industries, where the workers are represented, not only on the *Aufsichtsrat* but on the *Vorstand* as well, by the personnel director, who can be appointed and dismissed only with the approval of the workers' representatives on the *Aufsichtsrat*. The workers' representation on the *Aufsichtsrat*, which in these industries is 50 per cent, is partly in the hands of the unions alone, and partly by the unions acting with the works councils.

The biggest question overhanging industrial relations in 1968 was whether this form of co-determination, as practised in coal, iron and steel, should be extended to the rest of industry. The unions have launched a great campaign in favour of extension, on the ground that industrial democracy is not complete without it. The employers are resisting on the ground that, as it is they who take the risk in industry, it is they who should make the decisions. Parliament will be called upon to discuss and settle the issue.

Employer organisations are the Confederation of German Employers' Associations and the Federation of German Industries. The former includes all employers in trade, industry, commerce, banking, etc., while the second includes industrial employers only. While the main concern of the Confederation is to act, through its member organisations, as the negotiating partner of the trade unions in wage agreements, the Federation seeks mainly to evolve a joint policy among its members on such matters as taxation and cartel law. It seeks also to promote the interests of its members in parliament, and has some 100 committees and sub-committees for consulting and advising members on every aspect of foreign trade, etc.

The Confederation has no executive functions in wage negotiations, but acts in a general advisory capacity. It is organised firstly on a geographical basis, with a branch in each of the federal states, secondly according to trades and industry. Thus there is in each of the federal states a branch of the Confederation, each with a number of affiliated units or members, and also an organisation representing each individual branch of industry, trade and commerce. It is the state branch of each industry (e.g. the Bavarian branch of the building employers) which negotiates directly with the builders' union on wage agreements.

Some 90 per cent of all industry, trade and commerce, ranging from mining to agriculture and including wholesale and retail trade, is included through about 400 local associations in the state branches, and through them again in the Confederation, which has its headquarters in Cologne. As well as with wages, the Confederation concerns itself with a large variety of subjects including unemployment insurance, occupational training, youth and welfare work, and matters that fall within the scope of the International Labour Organisation in Geneva.

EMPLOYMENT AND UNEMPLOYMENT

From 1948 onwards, when currency reform provided the basis from which economic recovery could proceed, the unemployed returning from the armed forces and prisoner of war camps and the expellees and refugees from the east began, with the rest of those needing work, to be absorbed into industry. By 1950 the unemployed figure was down to 10 per cent and by 1960, when the 'economic miracle' was at its height, to hardly more than 1 per cent. By 1962 it was down to 0.7 per cent and 'guest workers' were pouring in from Italy, Spain, Greece, Turkey and other countries to meet what had become an acute labour shortage on the West German market. Their numbers were, at the maximum, well over a million, though they sank during the recession of 1966-7 to under that figure. As recovery proceeded during 1968 they showed signs of returning. The flow of workers from East Germany was mainly political in its character—the workers and their families were fleeing from the East German Communist régime—but it none the less served to ease the shortage on the West German labour market. The flow ended abruptly in August 1961, when the Communists erected their dividing wall across Berlin. Unemployment during the recession reached a maximum of 674,000 in February 1967, but by September of the same year it was down to 340,000 and by mid-1968 to 264,000. Over seven million women in West Germany are gainfully employed. This is about a third of all employees.

TRADE FAIRS AND EXHIBITIONS

A total of between forty and fifty trade fairs and exhibitions are held in West Germany, most of them annually, though a few are biannual and some, such as women's underwear, are held four times a year. They are all of supra-regional or international importance, though the Hanover fair is the largest and best-known. Its main emphasis is on capital goods of all kinds, though consumer goods for export are also shown. Every second year an international air show is included.

Frankfurt is famous for its spring and autumn fairs, which display domestic textiles, arts and crafts, musical instruments and stationery. Frankfurt also holds an international book fair, a motor show and others. Cologne specialises in consumer goods, including household effects and hardware, clothing, food and drink, sports goods and photographic equipment. In Düsseldorf there are the printing and paper, automation and electronics fairs and others. Munich holds building machinery and international handicrafts fairs, while West Berlin is famous for its annual agricultural fair known as the 'Green Week.' Nüremberg is famous for its toy fair, Hamburg for boats, textiles and foodstuffs, Offenbach for leather goods and Stuttgart for oil and heating equipment.

FOREIGN TRADE

With production at a standstill after the war, West Germany had no means of exporting in order to pay for necessary food imports. Trade deficits that amounted, for example, in 1950 to £255 million=$710 million were covered by American gifts and credits that took the form from 1948 onwards of the generous Marshall Plan. It was this American aid as much as the energies and abilities of the German people and the liberal policies of Dr Erhard, the Minister of Economics, that laid the foundations of the famous German 'economic miracle.' The economic recovery stemmed also from the indispensable currency reform of 1948 which put an end to the wild inflation of the previous years in which for most purposes black market cigarettes had taken the place of the worthless paper currency. Another important year was 1958 when the West German currency was, like most others in western Europe, made fully convertible. West German foreign trade increased during these years and in the early sixties overtook Britain's, which had held second place in the world after America. By 1965 America had 13.4 per cent of the total, West Germany 10.2 per cent and Britain 9.1 per cent. West Germany's trade has been much stimulated by her membership of the Common Market.

Since 1952, when the deficit of previous years turned for the first time into a surplus (£60 million=$183 million), progress has been irregular, but there has always been a surplus of larger or smaller proportions. In 1967 West Germany was helped out of its economic recession by the very large export surplus of £1,545 million=$4,250 million.

West Germany's main exports are engineering products of a wide range, including much machinery, both heavy and light. They amount to 21 per cent of total exports. Motor vehicles come next with 14 per cent and chemical products third with 13. Electrical products, iron and steel, general hardware, textiles and other exports range from 9 per cent (electrical products) to 2 per cent (food products). Chief imports are foodstuffs, including conventional necessities (coffee, tea, etc.), at 9 per cent, non-ferrous metals and semi-finished products 7 per cent, textiles, engineering products, chemical products, crude oil and natural gas, etc., in decreasing order, down to building materials at under 2 per cent.

The above figures show that, as compared with pre-war, exports have remained mainly industrial goods, while on the import side foodstuffs have given way largely to industrial and semi-manufactured goods. Imports cover a wider range than exports, with no single category of goods approaching the big export categories, e.g. of cars, chemicals, etc., in either volume or value.

The United States stands at the head of the list of countries from which West Germany draws imports. The figure of 13 per cent (1965) was followed by France with 11 per cent, while Britain was sixth with 4.5 per cent. On the export side France was first with 11 per cent, Holland second with 10 per cent and the United States third with 8 per cent. Britain was ninth with 4 per cent.

West Germany's trade with eastern block countries amounts to only about 4 per cent of its total trade and it grows only very slowly. Imports were in 1965 £260 million=$730 million, compared with exports of £240 million=$670 million. The chief trading partner for both imports and exports was Russia, followed at some distance by Poland.

Imports increased sixfold between 1950 and 1967, to reach a total of £6,316 million=$17,545 million. Exports increased tenfold over the same period, to a total of £7,834 million=$21,761 million.

The large export surpluses have been used to cover the cost of such conventional invisible imports as shipping, insurance, tourist expenditure, etc., and the less usual one of remittances sent home by the large number of foreign workers. Tourists and foreign workers together took or sent £567 million=$1,575 million out of the country in 1967.

Two other special items in the final West German balance are the invisible exports represented by the expenditure of allied (mostly American) troops in Germany. The figure for 1965 was £375 million=$1,050 million. Then there have been over the years the arms purchases made by West Germany in America and Britain, which have largely offset the total cost to the countries of keeping troops on West German soil. These purchases have been supplemented in recent years by the purchase of American and British state securities. Even so, the cost to the two countries of stationing troops in West Germany has not been fully covered.

It is not easy to select a figure which shows realistically the final position after all payments to and from the country have been made—i.e. the balance of payments. A figure much used in all countries is the rise or fall in the reserves of the central bank, but this can in certain circumstances be misleading—e.g. if there have been movements of short-term capital ('hot money,' very often, which is seeking shelter from some temporarily depressed financial centre elsewhere). If these short term capital movements are omitted the result may be the more realistic 'basic balance,' as it is called, and if all capital movements are omitted the 'balance on current account' remains.

Bearing these definitions in mind, it may be said that the finally favourable figures that had become familiar in West Germany for a decade or so were interrupted in 1965. In that year the balance on current account showed a deficit of £540 million=$1,525 million, which meant that the favourable balance of trade of £455 million=$1,275 million had been more than cancelled out by the invisible items named above. But to set against this there was a net import of capital of £240 million=$675 million, so that the final fall in Bundesbank reserves was kept to a relatively modest £134 million=$375 million. In 1966 the reserves rose by £92.7 million=$275 million as compared with 1965, and in 1967 by £37.1 million=$103 million over 1966. Total reserves at the end of 1967 stood at £2,727 million=$7,575 million.

This recovery, together with the generally favourable outlook for 1968, was accompanied by continuing weakness in the final balances of other countries (in particular Britain, with its similar economy, but including also America), and by the prospect, following the unrest and strikes, of weakness in France. The result was a renewed call in some international circles for a revaluation of the DM—which would have the effect of reducing West Germany's exports and hence its favourable balance of trade. The West German authorities declared themselves unwilling to accept such a braking of their new forward movement, but hoped to satisfy international opinion by exporting capital—especially in the form of aid to developing countries. In this they succeeded to the point where, in 1967, they passed Britain for the first time, to become third in the list of countries providing aid. First, as always, was America, followed by France. West Germany came next with nearly £65 million=$180 million, while Britain was fourth with rather less.

West Germany, at the time of the currency crisis of November 1968, was put under great pressure by Britain, America and France to revalue its currency. But it refused for a variety of reasons, of which one of the most important was that, only a few days before the meeting in Bonn of the Finance Ministers and Central Bank chiefs of the main countries concerned, it had announced what amounted to a 'concealed' revaluation. This took the form of a 4 per cent surcharge on exports (it was West Germany's vast export surplus that had given rise to criticism) and a corresponding 4 per cent rebate on import levies. At the Bonn conference itself, Bonn also emerged as the biggest contributor to the £800 million=$2,000 million international stand-by loan in support of the franc.

FINANCE

At the head of the banking system is the *Bundesbank* (Federal

Bank), which performs broadly the same functions as the Bank of England, the Federal Bank of America and central banks everywhere. It is the bank of note issue, the government banker, generally the manager of the entire financial system of the country, and the custodian of its gold and currency reserves. It is not, however, a government-controlled bank like the Bank of England, and indeed its charter guarantees its independence of the government. The fact that it exercises this was seen during the economic recession of 1966-7, when it ignored not the government's order—for it would never be so foolish as to challenge the bank by giving one—but at least the government's known wish to have the bank rate lowered and credit restrictions generally relaxed. The rate finally did come down, by stages from 5 per cent to 3 in May 1967, and other forms of the credit squeeze were relaxed, but only in the bank's good time. It was given its independent position in order to avoid the danger that, like the *Reichsbank* during the Nazi period, it might become the mere instrument of government policy. The *Bundesbank* is accordingly highly respected by the public, as well as in financial circles at home and abroad, and is recognised as having played a key part in preserving the stability of the currency. In view of the federal nature of the West German constitution, and the independent position of the state authorities, there is a branch of the *Bundesbank* in each state, whose task is to ensure co-ordination.

The gold and currency reserves (mainly dollars and sterling) of any central bank are one of the key indicators of the financial standing of the country concerned, and after wartime loss these have been built up steadily again in West Germany. They have indeed enabled the country to play a vital part in international financial affairs—in particular in shoring up weak currencies (see this chapter—Currency). They stood at a total in the *Bundesbank* at the end of 1965 of £2,750 million=$7,200 million, and have risen since then by about £180 million=$500 million (early 1968).

Ordinary banking business is conducted by 12,700 joint-stock banks, private banks and other financial institutions, of which the 'big three' are the *Deutsche Bank*, the *Dresdner Bank* and the *Commerz Bank*. The fourth largest is the trade union *Bank für Gemeinwirtschaft*. There are also specialised banks such as the German Municipal Bank, the Agricultural Annuity Bank, The Equalisation of Burdens Bank and the Raiffeisen Bank.

Of these, the Equalisation of Burdens Bank (*Lastenausgleichsbank*) is probably unique to West Germany, since its exists to deal with the financial side of the aid that has been given to the country's millions of expellee population (see Chapter I—Population). These people arrived from the eastern part of the country, not only after distressing experiences, but almost totally without property. The government took the view that less unfortunate members of the community could reasonably be called on to aid them financially, and imposed a 50 per cent levy on property (valued at the date of the currency reform, 20 June 1948), and by the end of 1967 a total of £6,030 million=$16,750 million had been paid out through the *Lastenausgleichsbank* under a large number of headings. They included cash payments, housing aid, special hardship payments, war damage pensions, compensation for loss of former savings, loss on currency exchange, loans, training aid, etc. Most of the claims, which amount to a total of about £9,000 million=$25,000 million, will have been met by 1970, though some, in the form of pensions, will go on well beyond the year 2,000.

The Raiffeisen Bank, of which there are 14,000 branches, mainly in the rural areas of the country and in the smaller towns, is named after Friedrich Raiffeisen, the nineteenth-century pioneer who brought agricultural co-operatives to Germany. They have played a most valuable part in providing the agricultural community—especially the smaller farmers—with sound financial foundations. Through the co-operatives which operate through the Raiffeisen banks, the farmer is able to buy his seed, agricultural machinery, fuel, etc., on far more advantageous terms than he could get for himself. Through the co-operatives he is also enabled to sell his produce collectively, and thus more rationally and simply than he could do it alone. The Raiffeisen banks administer total deposits of £2,300 million=$6,500 million.

The banks in West Germany play a far bigger part than in Britain and America in stock exchange business. Instead of going to a broker (*Makler*) when he wants to buy stocks or shares, the ordinary buyer goes to the bank. Business direct with the broker is thus limited to banks and other professional operators. The banks also hold securities on behalf of the ordinary individual, sending him an annual account and charging a small fee.

Stock exchange business is not so centralised in West Germany (because of the regional character of the country) as it is on the London Stock Exchange or on the Paris *Bourse* or even in the much larger Wall Street. There are important stock exchanges, not only in Berlin (West), the former capital, but also in Bremen, Düsseldorf, Hamburg, Hanover, Munich and Stuttgart. There is no exchange in Bonn, the present capital. At the end of 1965 the par value of stocks and shares was £4,100 million=$11,475 million, and the total value of dividends distributed by 1,630 joint-stock companies with a share capital of £3,190 million= $8,940 million was about £357 million=$1,000 million. The average dividend of all companies was 13.47 per cent and the yield 3.98 per cent. The index of share prices, with the end of December 1953 as the base (100), had risen to 822 by August 1960, which was about the high point of the 'economic miracle' boom, but had dropped to 562 by the end of December 1964 and to 474 by October 1965. It has since risen again to 578 (mid-1968).

West Germany in the mid-sixties was justly regarded as a rich and prosperous country with reserves of gold and currency in the *Bundesbank* higher than in most countries other than America. But this 'ready cash' position should not be allowed to obscure the fact that, when long-term assets are considered as well, West Germany is not so much better off than Britain as is often supposed. West Germany might be (and sometimes is) likened to a well-to-do young man with a pocket full of money as compared with an elderly gentleman who does not quite know where his next meal is coming from, even though he has vast capital locked up in real estate. Long-term West German investments abroad rise continuously (e.g. by £277 million=$775 million in 1965), but they are still not comparable with those of Britain, and still less of America. For example, while the total foreign investment of British private persons had by 1967 reached about £10,000 million, the comparable figure for Germans was about £1,700 million. In short, the notorious balance of payments problems of Britain, and above all those of America, should be regarded as temporary embarrassments rather than as proof that either of those countries are being economically outstripped by West Germany. Thus it remains true in West Germany that capital—above all long-term capital—is harder to raise on the public market than in either London or New York, and the banks are therefore left in a key position as the source of such funds. They have very large (often a controlling proportion) of funds in important industrial undertakings, and at the beginning of 1967 their shorter and medium-term credits to industry and public and private borrowers stood at £27,800 million=$78,100 million.

At the top of the Zugspitze in Bavaria—Germany's highest mountain.

Carnival time in Bavaria.

6

How They Learn

THE BASIC policy of the German state has always been to leave education, and cultural affairs generally, to develop in their own way. But in common with most other states it has none the less taken such basic steps as to make education compulsory and to provide considerable funds. Most schools and universities in the West Germany of today are state institutions, and teachers

---

The August Thyssen headquarters in Düsseldorf.

Rothenburg ob der Tauber (above the Tauber).

and professors are for the most part civil servants. Organisations for scientific and other research, such as the Max Planck Society and the German Research Association, take the legal form of the 'registered society,' which means that, although organised independently, they are financed by the state. There are in addition such private foundations for research as the Volkswagen Foundation, the Fritz Thyssen Foundation and, in late 1968 not yet fully-established, the Krupp Foundation. These correspond to the great foundations in America that endow scientific research.

It follows from the German tradition and from the federal character of the present West German constitution that cultural affairs—including education in all its forms—are in the main within the responsibility of the states. There is a minister of cultural affairs in every state government (a senator in the city states), but none in the federal government in Bonn. In order that the consequence of state independence should not be a fragmentation of the educational system, in which each state went its own way, a permanent conference of the ministers of culture was set up in 1949. Although only an advisory body, the conference has been able to keep state cultural policy on roughly uniform lines. It stands outside the general framework of the constitution, and is entirely outside the control of the federal government, yet cultural policy in West Germany would be almost inconceivable without it.

Schooling in Germany has a tradition that goes back more than eleven hundred years, and in some German states it was made compulsory in the eighteenth century. Since the middle of the nineteenth century it has been compulsory throughout the country. The basic principles of the system set up under the constitution of 1949 were that education should be under the general supervision of the state governments, that persons entitled to control the upbringing of a child (i.e. parents or guardians) should decide whether or not it should receive religious instruction and if so of what kind, and that religious instruction should form part of the curriculum in all state schools. The right to establish private schools was guaranteed, provided that they were state-approved and supervised. There are not many such schools in West Germany, but they include the well-known one at Salem, near Lake Constance, where Prince Philip was in part educated and at whose sister foundation at Gordonstoun the Prince of Wales was a pupil.

Education may begin voluntarily (e.g. in *Kindergarten*) at the age of three or four, as the parents may decide, but compulsorily it begins at the age of six in a primary school (*Volksschule*). All children must remain there for a minimum of four years, but since education in some form is compulsory until the age of eighteen, it is not then ended. Almost 80 per cent in fact remain at the primary school, which provides basic general education until the age of fourteen to fifteen, and then go on to a vocational school (see below). The remaining 20 per cent who show themselves by examination capable of profiting by it, go on to the intermediate school (*Mittelschule*) or to the high school (*Gymnasium*).

Primary and vocational education is free, but from then on payment adjusted to the means of the parents may be required. Scholarships and grants are on such a scale that few, if any, pupils capable of benefiting from higher education are barred from it.

In the intermediate schools one foreign language is compulsory, and the pupils then usually go on to middle-grade posts in industry or commerce, or to further, though vocational, instruction in advanced professional schools (*Fachschulen*). Education at the *Gymnasium* is for nine years, and the certificate (*Reifeprüfung*) with which it ends opens the way to the university. There are three types of *Gymnasium*, of which one specialises in the classical languages, the second in modern languages, and the third in mathematics and science. Even if the *Gymnasium* pupil does not go on to the university—and many do not—he is qualified at the end of his studies for the higher posts in commerce or the civil service or for entry into one of the professions. In 1965 the number of pupils in *Volksschulen* was 5,575,700; in *Mittelschulen* 570,900 and in *Gymnasien* 957,900. The number of pupils per class in *Volksschulen* was on an average 35; in *Mittelschulen* 33 and in *Gymnasien* 28. The total public cost in 1961 of *Volksschulen* was £417 million=$1,168 million; of *Mittelschulen* £44 million=$124 million. The cost per head at a *Volksschule* was £73=$205; at a *Mittelschule* £122=$340; and at a *Gymnasium* £182=$510. Public expenditure on education amounts to about 7 per cent of the total.

In the past, schools were invariably confessional—meaning that either Catholic or Protestant religious instruction was given. There is now a trend towards the non-confessional school for both Catholics and Protestants, and indeed for children of any creed whatever. But this is a much-disputed field, in which change is far more rapid in some states than in others. In some there is strong resistance to change of any kind, and it will be long before uniformity is reached.

The great majority of West German children complete their primary education at the *Volksschule* at the age of fifteen, and start at that age to earn their living, but they are none the less required by law to attend vocational schools (*Berufsschulen*) on a part-time basis for a further three years. Employers and parents alike see that they attend on one or two days a week to receive a total of nine to twelve hours' instruction in both the theory and practise of some trade or craft. General education is also continued. Trade, business, farming, mining, housekeeping are among the wide variety of subjects studied and practised with the aid of facilities—workshops, kitchens, etc., provided by the schools. Each pupil is given a certificate at the end of his three years' attendance at the vocational school.

Side by side with the vocational school is the specialised vocation school which gives more intensive instruction in a variety of subjects, including commerce, administration, handicrafts and physical training. Entry may be from the *Mittelschulen* as well as from *Volksschulen*, and courses last from one to three years. A majority of the pupils are girls training in nursing, care of children, domestic science and other specifically feminine subjects. For boys there may be the processing of precious metals, industrial art, applied graphics, musical instrument making, etc.

In still more specialised schools training is available for the theatre, ballet, music or art.

There are twenty-one universities in West Germany, including such ancient and famous foundations as Heidelberg and Göttingen. In addition there are nine technical colleges and five technical institutes of university rank. Four more universities are planned or already in part functioning.

But, partly because of the growing demand for university education, and partly because of the German tradition which allows those students who desire, and have the means, to remain at the university indefinitely, there is still a shortage. This, combined with teaching methods and administration that have been the subject of growing criticism, has led to the kind of student unrest, and indeed occasional violence, that exists in many western countries and that has become at least in part political in character. University reform is constantly discussed and planned, but so far (late 1968) there has been no decisive action. At the head of the university system is the rectors' conference which concerns itself with co-ordination and the discussion of common problems. Its members are the rectors (principals) of the universities and technical colleges.

There are about 265,000 students at West German universities and other institutes of higher education, including about 22,000 foreigners. More than half are in the arts faculties, about 15 per cent each in the medical and natural science faculties, and the rest in technology. Almost 25 per cent of all students are women. Of the parents of students, about 35 per cent are in academic professions, 32 per cent are civil servants, 30 per cent are office workers of a wide variety of kinds and 5 per cent are manual workers. About 12 per cent of students finance their studies from their own earnings, and about $1\frac{1}{2}$ per cent from their own unearned property. Some 18 per cent receive monthly grants up to £26=$72.50 (the amount is discussed annually and usually raised) from a fund set up in 1957 by the federal and state governments, while particularly gifted students receive special grants from a second fund, to which, besides the federal and state authorities, other organisations such as the

Volkswagen Foundation contribute. Roughly 40 per cent of all students receive aid from either public or private sources. The average cost to the public authorities of every student is about £635=$1,750 a year. About 35,000 students a year receive university qualifications, of which 80 per cent are state diplomas, 17 per cent are state diplomas plus doctorates, and the remaining 3 per cent are doctorates only. Some 7,500 students fail their final examinations.

West German universities are not of the Oxford and Cambridge type, with residential colleges. Students live in hostels or in private accommodation provided by the authorities or found by themselves. Nor is there, except for those studying for a doctorate, the tutorial system which brings the student into direct personal contact with the supervisor of his studies. Important grievances contributing to the present student discontents might have been avoided if there had been such a system, since students tend to claim that all that is expected of them is that they should attend lectures—much as if they were still at school listening to a teacher.

But what West German students do have in a more developed form than in many countries—though they say it is still not enough—is the legal right to participate through their student parliament and executive in university administration. Details vary widely as between one university and another. They also have in some universities their corporations (*Korporationen*), which are legally recognised and which occupy themselves with the welfare of their members, with cultural matters, travel arrangements, and above all with assisting their members to find employment, when they leave the university, which is appropriate to their station in life—for the corporations smack strongly of snobbery. There is in fact something about them that suggests the freemasonry of the British 'old school tie' system— meaning that members of socially smart corporations can count on social and professional aid from 'old boy' members already well-established in life. The student corporations with, in some cases, their coloured caps, were once legendary for their duelling and drinking. Neither of these activities belong entirely to the past, though duelling is practised only on a limited scale and in strict privacy in those universities where it is allowed or tolerated.

7

How They Get About

A MINISTRY OF TRANSPORT was set up in West Germany in 1949 to co-ordinate the work of the local authorities, who were at that stage engaged on the giant task of making good wartime damage. But the ministry was also charged with leading and directing the work of bringing the transport system, whether by water, rail or road, technically up to date and keeping it abreast of new developments. Although work on militarily useful projects such as the *Autobahn* had been pushed ahead during the war, most of the rest of the road and rail systems and the inland waterways had been neglected, and civil air transport had come to a complete stop. This was not restarted until August 1954, when the allies relinquished the air control they had taken over entirely at the end of the war. They took this step in anticipation of the restoration of sovereignty that was to follow in May 1955. The ministry also has certain responsibility in the field of shipping (safety regulations, etc.). It has supervised the investment of vast sums in the transport system over the years, including £1,333 million=$3,750 million in 1967. As a consequence, West Germany can fairly claim to have as modern and efficient a transport system, both on the surface and in the air, as any in Europe.

RAILWAYS

The railway system is in the main state-owned and run,

and is known as the *Bundesbahn* (Federal Railway). The length of its operational track is nearly 19,000 miles, of which over 4,000 are electrified. Under existing plans some 4,000 miles of little-used and unprofitable track are to be closed down, but electrification of the rest will be pushed ahead until complete. In addition to the *Bundesbahn* there are some 150 small commercially-owned networks (e.g. on Lüneburg Heath), operating 3,107 miles of track.

The number of passengers carried in 1965 was 1,060 million, of whom 582 million travelled on cheap workers' or children's tickets. Many others enjoyed reductions for various reasons—for example, under a scheme introduced for a limited period in late 1968 a wife travelling with her husband or vice versa paid only half-fare—and only one in three paid the full fare. *Bundesbahn* publicity, aimed at stimulating passenger travel, is good and lively, especially in the holiday season when such posters appear as 'Take a holiday from your car—go by rail,' and innumerable special offers are made, including 'afternoon coffee excursions' on a round trip basis to places of tourist interest. The *Bundesbahn* has always stoutly resisted the defeatist view that, in the motor-car and aeroplane age, railways are on their way out and can do no more than accept their fate. Trains are in the main punctual, especially the crack expresses that invariably arrive on the minute. The TEE (Trans European Express) trains link up with neighbouring countries and the 'F' (*Fern*—long distance) trains have, as well as restaurant cars and sleepers, special compartments for bars, telephone, writing facilities and secretaries. A few have observation cars for the better enjoyment of the scenery, and some are romantically named—Rheingold, Parsifal, Helvetia, etc. (for the supplements chargeable on these trains see Chapter IX.)

Freight carried in 1965 was 317 million tons, and the number of persons employed by the *Bundesbahn* was 448,000. By the end of 1967 the payroll had declined, as a result of rationalisation and modernisation, to 414,000 and it is still falling steadily. One form of rationalisation visible to travellers, and much welcomed by them, has been the steady decline in the number of ticket-collectors at barriers. By the end of 1968 only 6 per cent of all stations were still manned at the barriers and most of these only at intervals. But the transfer of all ticket-control duties to conductors on the trains has not meant redundancy for the men formerly at the barriers. The present position has been reached simply by not replacing them as they have retired.

Like the state railways in most countries, the *Bundesbahn* works at a loss. It amounted to £143 million=$394 million in 1967, which was £42.3 million=$117.5 million more than the previous year. But in 1968 it fell by £11.4 million=$31 million. This was a result of an increase in income from both passenger and freight services, and certainly in the case of freight this trend is likely to continue when, as is expected, the ministry of transport's great new plan for modernising the country's transport system becomes law. Much freight will, under the plan, be diverted from the overburdened roads to the underburdened railways, to the advantage of all concerned except the road haulage firms, who have protested loudly and who have succeeded in getting the plan modified in their favour. But the federal government is also to spend much money on stimulating combined road-rail transport, with trucks riding pick-a-back on trains. An entirely new company known as 'Combi-Trans' is to be set up. The *Bundesbahn* itself plans a national container company with sixty terminals for the new-style carriage of goods in handy containers. By the end of 1969 thirty of these are expected to be in operation. The new service will be on a door-to-door basis, and much is expected of it. Another development, much welcomed by motorists who dislike long approach drives to their final holiday or other destinations, is the service in which cars are carried by train. The driver dines and sleeps aboard and sets off fresh the next morning at the wheel.

Besides the *Bundesbahn* and the small but not unimportant commercial railways, there have long been underground and surface electric services in Berlin and Hamburg. The first sections of the first underground railways to be built since the war came into service in Frankfurt, Cologne and Munich in late 1968. These new developments are an indication of the growing number of those who commute between their homes and their offices or factories. But, since there are no great cities comparable in size with London or New York, the commuter problem will remain relatively small. Many thousands of West Germans travel up to ten or fifteen miles from their work, but there are few if any who live so far from it as those London office workers who commute from Brighton, or the New Yorkers who commute from Nyack.

ROADS

The autobahn network has been much extended since the war. The length in use when work re-started in 1949 was 1,322 miles; by 1967 it was 2,179 miles. A further 559 miles were under construction, and 1,926 miles were in the planning stage. It is now possible to drive from Hamburg in the north to Munich or Basle (Switzerland) in the south without ever leaving the autobahn. A spur in the north connects West Germany with Scandinavia, while in the west there are autobahn links with Holland and Belgium. The division of the country makes extension to the east impracticable, though the pre-war autobahn connections with Berlin and Leipzig are in limited use.

The autobahns are magnificent in design and construction. They sweep the countryside in harmonious curves, they cross rivers and deep gorges and pierce mountains. They are themselves crossed overhead by the bridges of local roads, which are of varying architectural styles so that monotony is avoided. The autobahns are free of disfiguring advertisement hoardings. A few sections in traffic-dense areas have three traffic lanes in each direction. Other main roads (*Bundesstrassen*) are being rapidly modernised after wartime neglect. Minor roads are not up to the British or American standard but are also being improved. The length of classified roads, including autobahns, is 96,239 miles, of which 18,557 miles (often on flyovers) are inside built-up areas.

The rapid growth of road traffic is shown by the figures. For all vehicles taken together they were 1.5 million in 1949 and 13.7 million (excluding light motorcycles) in 1967. This gives a ratio of about five inhabitants per vehicle, which is roughly the same as for Britain. For America it is about two. The number of vehicles per square mile is, at over a hundred, about the same in West Germany and Britain, while in the vastly bigger area of America it is hardly a score. The number of persons killed in road accidents stands now (1968) at over 16,000, which in relation to traffic density is the highest figure in the world. Nearly one bed in two in hospital surgical wards is occupied by someone injured in a road accident and 45 per cent of all court cases are concerned with traffic offences.

As well as ordinary private and commercial vehicles on West German roads there are municipal trams, buses, trolley-buses and passenger buses run by the federal railways and federal post authorities. The trams are tending to disappear from the centres of big cities, but are still extensively used in smaller towns like Bonn for both inner-town and inter-town traffic. The railway and post buses are used mainly in country areas. They do not compete with municipal transport inside towns and cities.

Parking is as much a problem in West Germany as in all other highly motorised countries, and the authorities have been no more successful than others in solving it. More space is constantly being provided in the bigger towns, both in underground and skyscraper garages, but there is never enough. On the streets a growing number of parking meters seeks either to scare the motorist off or at least limit his stay. Signs put up by the police ban parking entirely on considerable stretches of street. In the absence of any indication to the contrary the motorist may park on the right hand side of any public highway (left hand as well on one-way streets). He may even have two wheels (occasionally all four) on the pavement if there is a white line to mark the limit.

WATERWAYS

The most important waterways are the Rhine and its tributaries (the Moselle, the Main, the Neckar and some smaller ones), and the network of canals between the industrial Ruhr and Emden. The Rhine-Main-Danube canal, now under construction, will enable shipping to travel from the North Sea to the Black Sea. The cost of constructing the 421 miles that lie within West German territory will be about £134 million=$375 million. The total present length of navigable inland waterways is 3,728 miles, of which 1,151 miles are canals. The Rhine is navigable for a length of 406 miles.

The inland fleet consists (1966) of 7,612 cargo vessels and 595 passenger ships. Of the total fleet, 73 per cent is motorised. Cargo handled at inland river ports in 1965 was 287 million tons, of which 32 million tons was at Duisburg, the biggest inland port in Europe.

AIR TRAFFIC

The West German airline, Lufthansa, is 75 per cent state-financed, with the rest of the shares in the hands of the public. The government is often assumed to be able to influence its decisions—for example, in the matter of whether American, British or other aircraft are to be bought—but the Lufthansa is entitled to run itself on independent, commercial lines, and firmly resists all forms of pressure. Its air fleet is in fact almost entirely American, though after much hesitation it now seems likely to take options on the 'airbus' conceived as Anglo-German-French until the British withdrew in mid-1969.

Lufthansa carried 4,285 million passengers in 1967, which was 17 per cent more than in the previous year. Its freight tonnage also rose by 4 per cent to a total of 24,100 tons. Lufthansa planes fly to seventy-eight airports in fifty-two countries. On the North Atlantic route they have 132 scheduled flights a week. Frankfurt is the third largest airport in Europe, with a staff of 10,000. Efficiency and comfort are up to the highest international standards, and the service is being constantly extended and improved.

8

How They Amuse Themselves

GERMANS ARE sometimes regarded as a grim-faced, humourless people, with little, if any, of the capacity for laughter and the lighter side of life that is held to be characteristic of the Latin races, especially perhaps of the Italians. Apart from the difficulty (discussed in Chapter I—National Characteristics) of making such widespread judgements about either the Germans or anyone else, it must be said that this particular one is untrue even of the north Germans, of whom it is most often said.

Rhinelanders are gay to the point of fecklessness, Bavarians are ruggedly jovial, and these qualities are fully revealed in what in the Rhineland is called carnival and in Bavaria *Fasching*. This is the period of both public and private festivity that begins after Christmas and goes on non-stop until the final days before Lent, when it rises to a tremendous culmination. On *Rosenmontag* (the Monday before Shrove Tuesday) there are processions through the streets, in which huge plaster figures on motorised floats guy the political and other personalities and events of the year. All business, official, public and private, is at a standstill, everyone turns out in the street in fancy dress, and all normal inhibitions about addressing strangers of either sex disappear. The Rhineland and Bavaria, it should be noted, are the main Catholic areas of Germany, and it is almost exclusively there that the old pagan festivities, in which winter was driven out and spring welcomed, have been taken over.

But if it should be objected that carnival and *Fasching* are regional amusements and therefore not typical, there are others

How They Amuse Themselves

that cover the country. One of these is in the *Kegelbahn* (bowling alley), which was a tradition in Germany long before it became a post-war craze everywhere, and the other is at the *Schützenfest* (marksman's festival), where marksmanship is practised throughout the year with small-bore rifles, and where a *Schützenkönig* is chosen by competition at the annual *Fest*, where gay costumes are worn and where, as well as marksmanship, there is much beer-drinking and jollification.

Apart from the fun and games, these two peculiarly German forms of amusement have considerable social and indeed democratic value in that the members of the *Kegelklub* (bowling club) and the *Schützenverein* (marksman's society) are often drawn from a wide range of social classes. The local doctor and lawyer will be found bowling away on *Kegel* evening with the local garage hand or house painter or factory hand, entirely regardless of social differences. Business or 'shop' talk of every kind will be banned, and the entire club will once a year finance a week's holiday for itself from the 'kitty,' into which the losers have regularly paid.

There is also the very German institution of the *Stammtisch*, which means literally 'tribal table,' though it is in practice a meeting of regulars—perhaps originally tribal elders at the local beer house or *Kneipe* (pub). There are few German men—for it is an essentially male activity—who do not meet with up to a dozen or so of their friends at their *Stammtisch*, and indeed in many *Kneipen* a table will be reserved for them. Sport, politics, local gossip are all thoroughly discussed over beer and schnaps. The *Stammtisch* is traditionally a male institution, but the *Stammtisch* for ladies, and for that matter the *Kegelklub* for ladies, are no longer entirely unknown. The *Kegelklub* is indeed occasionally mixed, though the ladies have not yet been permitted to share in the exclusive masculine conversation at the *Stammtisch*. Part of the *Stammtisch* tradition, in fact, is that it gives the man an evening off from the wife and family.

Equally widespread is the *Kirmes* or fair with swings and roundabouts and stalls of every kind; while found in similar form in most countries, it is especially popular in Germany.

Travelling fairs move about the countryside, advertising their coming in advance so that the whole village or small town knows and prepares. During the week or more of the fair, traffic is liable to be diverted and everyone takes part. In Munich and West Berlin the fair takes on the similar but vastly bigger and grander form of the *Oktoberfest* (October Festival) which is, however, held in September. In Munich, in particular, the *Oktoberfest*, with its colourful Bavarian costumes, is a great tourist attraction and statistics are always published afterwards on the thousands of gallons of beer consumed and the tons of sausage.

In the wine-producing areas—the Rhineland, the Moselle valley, the Palatinate and Baden—a *Winzerfest* (Wine Festival) is held at some point or other during the summer in every village. There is again much jollification, with dancing in the streets, and everyone, including passers-by, is welcome. There is also much drinking—though wine this time, instead of beer.

Then there are colourful traditional festivities of many kinds in many places. A typical one is the water tournament at Ulm, on the Danube, where, in the manner of knights of old on horseback, watermen in traditional costume mount the prows of their boats and try to dislodge each other into the river with the aid of long wooden lances. Spectators on the bank enjoy the fun—and consume beer and sausage as well. There are many other such folklore occasions, especially in the Black Forest and Bavaria, where much pride is taken in traditional customs and costumes.

THEATRE AND MUSIC

Besides these 'folksy' forms of amusement, Germans are great theatre-goers and music-lovers. Over 20 million visits a year are made to 135 theatres that are subsidised by either federal or state or municipal authorities, or to fifty-five others run on a private commercial basis. One of the happier results of the long division of Germany into hundreds of princely domains is that many of the princes left their private theatres to posterity. As the period in which they were built was mainly the eighteenth century, the architecture is a delightful baroque. There are seventy such theatres now in use, both for drama and music. Since the theatres, whether modern or municipal, whether subsidised or commercial or inherited from the princes, are scattered throughout the country, there is no such concentration either in the old capital Berlin or in the new capital Bonn as, for example, in London or Paris. Many of the theatres, especially the eighteenth-century ones, are used for the theatre and music festivals that are an important part of the West German season. From spring, through the summer and into the autumn, the local people and visitors have a wide choice in these festivals of classic and modern drama and music. The best known in the outside world are the Wagner Festival at Bayreuth and the Passion play (at ten-years intervals, next in 1970) at Oberammergau. But the visitor who fails to get a ticket for the first—and there is always a great run on them—or is in the country in the wrong year for the second, might well choose, say, Schwetzingen, near Heidelberg, where *A Midsummer Night's Dream* or a programme of chamber music against the exquisite background of the eighteenth-century theatre makes as agreeable an evening of its kind as could easily be obtained anywhere.

Germans are great lovers of Shakespeare, of whom they have brilliant translations, and of their own classics in both drama and music. Thus there is never any difficulty in seeing a fine performance of Goethe, Schiller or Lessing, or in hearing Beethoven, Bach, Mozart and much more. For modern drama and music they have relied mainly since the war on foreigners; Bernard Shaw is a great favourite, and modern American dramatists such as Thornton Wilder and Tennessee Williams are very popular. Carl Zuckmayer and Berthold Brecht have until recently been among the few post-war German dramatists, but others are now appearing. They include Gert Weymann, Michael Mansfeld, Peter Weiss and Rolf Hochhuth—author of the two controversial plays *The Deputy*, critical of the silence of Pope Pius XII during the Nazi persecution of the Jews, and *The*

Soldiers, alleging that the death of General Sikorski, the wartime Polish leader, in an air crash, was engineered by Winston Churchill.

Besides modern drama there is the modern music of Werner Egk, Carl Orff, Hindemith and Boris Blacher, etc. While the classics are particularly cultivated in the Beethoven Festival in Bonn and the Mozart Festival in Würzburg, both classical and modern music may be heard in the great Berlin and Weisbaden festivals. Modern music is specially cultivated at a number of places, for example, the festival of contemporary music at Donaueschingen.

But, as well as hearing others, Germans like to play and sing themselves. Amateur musicians are organised into groups and as church choirs and choral societies. There are also large numbers of police, miners' and works' bands.

Apart from the great artists from abroad who are engaged from time to time to sing in opera houses, there are nearly always a number of foreign singers in the country who have not yet made their name. The reason for this is that West Germany is one of the few countries—possibly the only one—in which an opera singer who is not yet established can none the less get the experience, and earn the money, that he needs. The provincial opera houses provide a training ground—and sometimes a springboard to fame—of a kind that is available neither in Britain nor America.

This is possible because far more public money is spent in subsidising the theatre in all its forms than in possibly any other country. The figure for theatres and opera houses together is some £40 million=$112.5 million a year, and it is provided from the resources of state and local government authorities. Season-ticket holders form the backbone of most audiences and provide a minimum guaranteed income. They are generally organised into theatre clubs attached to individual theatres, and are much supported by blocks of employees from local firms and by the churches. This financial aid from public resources springs from the view that the theatre is an essential public service—in much the same way as the (also subsidised) state railways. Every member of the community is entitled to be able to go to the theatre at a price he can afford, just as he is entitled to travel by train for a reasonable charge.

The biggest post-war theatrical success in West Germany was *My Fair Lady*, which was seen in West Berlin by nearly a million people in 1963 in over 500 performances. The smallest theatre—*Das Podest* in Mainz—holds 60 people. The biggest— the Opera House in Hamburg—holds 1,440. The average number of seats is 252.

Theatre-going is on a large scale, but it would be larger if more good actors and actresses were available. The number is only about 100 first-class performers. This is largely due to the loss of the Jewish community, which provided pre-war Germany with so many of its greatest artists. The small number are also needed in the rest of the German-speaking world (Austria and parts of Switzerland) and on radio and television. The greatest actors and actresses are loaned out to local companies—a system which makes it possible to see a fine performance in, say, Wolfsburg or Erlangen or Iserlohn as well as in Hamburg or Berlin or Munich. The repertory company with a changing programme is still predominant, but what is called the 'en suite' system, in which plays follow each other at six- to eight-week intervals, is gaining ground. The touring theatre is also tending to push out the permanent company at any one theatre.

FILMS

Germany's main pre-war film studios were in that part of Berlin which remained in the hands of the Russians and are thus lost to the post-war West German film industry. Another great loss was the many great film actors and actresses who emigrated before the war, of whom Marlene Dietrich is the most distinguished still alive, or were for political reasons obliged to give up their work. But new studios have been constructed since the war in West Berlin, Hamburg, Wiesbaden, Göttingen and Munich. The studio at Geiselgasteig in Bavaria is one of the biggest in Western Europe. Cost of production is high (about £89,000=$250,000 for a black and white feature film and half as much again for a colour one), and the audiences of East Germany and the territories held by Poland and Russia are lost. This was a great handicap to the industry, even before television came as a new and powerful competitor.

In these circumstances only 56 of the 373 films on offer in 1965 were West German productions. Three came from East Germany and the rest from abroad, mainly from America. West German films accounted in 1965 for rather less than a third of the takings of the 5,209 cinemas with their 2,142,644 seats. From the end of the war the number of cinema attendances rose to a peak of 818 million in 1956, when, because of television competition, they began to decline. They were down by 1965 to 320 million. In that year the gross takings of the cinemas was £59 million=$166 million, of which £2 million=$5.6 million went in entertainment tax.

In Mainz and Heidelberg people still go to the cinema twelve times a year, while the average for the whole country is just over five times. In 1956 it was sixteen times.

RADIO AND TELEVISION

Radio and television fall within the general competence of the state authorities, but this does not mean that they either control or run them. The states provide, through their legislation, the legal basis for the existence of broadcasting stations and their organisational form, which is that of non-profit-making, public corporations with a very high degree of independence. Political parties and other outside bodies, and at times even individuals, seek sometimes to exert influence—by complaining, for example, that they have not had as much time on the air or on the screen as they think they should have, or by claiming that some programme or other is tendentious. These efforts are occasionally successful, as when the producer of some controversial programme is changed in deference to outsiders, but in general radio and television stations put up a sturdy resistance to interference from outside.

The regional organisation of radio gives the listener with a good enough receiver a choice, at least in theory, of nine different programmes. But in practice there is much overlapping and exchange of programmes, so that the choice is not quite so wide. The original television programme was joined in 1963 by a second and in 1966 by a third, while since 1967 there have been some colour transmissions. The self-governing independence of radio and television is ensured through the broadcasting council on which public bodies and associations, including representatives of licence holders, sit; through the administrative council which watches over the general working of a station, and finally through the *Intendant* (manager), who is responsible for the day-to-day running of the station and its programme.

The radio and television stations derive the bulk of their income from the fees paid by licence holders who, in mid-1968, numbered 18,745,188 for radio and 14,336,379 for television. The fees are 4s=50 cents a month for radio, and 10s=$1.25 for television, but of this one-quarter of the radio fee and 27 per cent of the television fee go to the postal authorities who provide the technical facilities and collect the fees. There are no commercially-sponsored radio or television programmes of the American type, but advertisements are transmitted at intervals varying widely from station to station.

Programmes on both radio and television are co-ordinated through a body with the cumbersome title of Working Party of German Statutory Broadcasting Stations, and this ensures among other things that each regional station gets its share of the joint overall programme. Thus, at the top, North and West German Radio each get 22.5 per cent of the total time, while at the bottom Radio Bremen and Saarland Radio each get 3 per cent. West Germany is one of the twenty countries which take Eurovision programmes from time to time, and there are occasional direct links with the television networks of Austria and Switzerland. Most transmitting time on both radio and television is taken up by music and entertainment. Cultural themes account for about 15 per cent of the time, and topical programmes and news for some 30 per cent. All radio stations except Bremen transmit some twenty-five to forty minutes a day of regional programmes for their own areas.

Recognising the importance of addressing themselves to others besides their own people, the West German authorities have set up *Deutschlandfunk* (German Radio) and *Die Deutsche Welle* (The Voice of Germany). The task of the first is to address, in the appropriate languages, the rest of Europe, but above all the people of East Germany, for whom it provides an invaluable link with the west. West German television stations also beam programmes to audiences on the eastern side of the dividing line. This is a matter of great annoyance to the Communist authorities there, but there is little they can do to prevent it. Having provided their own people with television sets for the purpose of receiving their own propaganda, they find them also receiving 'the enemy's.' *Die Deutsche Welle* transmits news, commentaries, etc., in scores of languages to all parts of the world.

Finally, West German listeners can and do tune in to British and American radio stations broadcasting from within their country. RIAS (Radio in the American Sector) was set up by the American occupying authorities after the war in their sector of Berlin, but it has stayed on to provide the East German people with another link with the west. It is for them that its transmissions are meant in the main, but they are widely heard by West German audiences. Then there are British and American forces broadcasting stations, some of whose programmes are highly popular with West German audiences.

BOOKS

For all the surge of interest in radio and especially television in West Germany, as in other countries, from the moment it became available, and for all the fear that it would become a not altogether desirable craze, the fact is that a recent opinion poll showed that reading was the favourite spare-time occupation of

West Germans. Of the people questioned, 30 per cent put reading first, followed by work in the house and garden (24 per cent), walking and rambling (17 per cent) and sport (11 per cent). Radio and television came only fifth with 9 per cent.

But what it is that West Germans read is not so clear. Literature, like everything else in the field of culture, was blighted by the dead hand of the Nazis, so that writers who were not prepared to conform to Nazi standards were obliged either to emigrate or give up writing. Thus a generation grew up that hardly knew the names, and certainly not the works, of Thomas Mann, Hermann Hesse, Stefan Zweig, Franz Werfel, Carl Zuckmayer, Berthold Brecht and many others. Much has been done by publishers and by the German Academy of Language and Poetry (*Deutsche Akademie für Sprache und Dichtung*) to enable older people to catch up and younger ones to start making acquaintance with their own literature, but it cannot be doubted that there is still a gap.

Germans under the Nazis were similarly cut off from the literature of the outside world, but here, too, the gap is closing. The works of T. S. Eliot, Anouilh, Faulkner, Christopher Fry, Sartre, Ernest Hemingway, Garcia Lorca, Ezra Pound, Thornton Wilder, Tennessee Williams and many others are as well known to serious readers in West Germany as in any country. There are excellent translations of the works of all these writers, though many West Germans are able to read them in the original.

But as well as with the generation of writers—whether in German or other languages—that is passing, the present generation in West Germany is eager for contact with what is entirely post-Nazi. It took some time for the dead hand to recede so far into the past that it could be forgotten, but within the past few years there has been something like a genuine rebirth of German literature. The names of Günter Grass, Heinrich Böll, Uwe Johnson, Ernst Kreuder and Heinz Piontek have given German writing a new reputation internationally, as well as inside West Germany and the rest of the German-speaking world. The memory of the past is still vivid in such documentary writings as Theodor Plievier's *Stalingrad* and Peter Bamm's *The Invisible Flag*.

Germans claim that it was in their country that book societies originated. Whether or not this is true, there are now twenty of them with some four million members. There are also 8,050 bookshops and 1,655 book-selling agencies and lending libraries. Many of the retail booksellers organise poetry-readings, lectures and special book displays.

MUSEUMS AND ART GALLERIES

Of Germany's 395 pre-war museums, 108 were destroyed completely during the hostilities and 149 were badly damaged. But this, happily, did not mean that their treasures were lost. Most had been removed in advance to places of safety. Since the war, old museums have been rebuilt and new ones added, so that the total is now 431 in 210 different places. One of the most celebrated art treasures in the world—the head of Nefertiti from the tomb of Tutankhamen—is in the West Berlin gallery, and there and in Munich and elsewhere are picture collections as fine as any in the world. There are also a number of private collections of great importance, including in particular the great collection of Meissen china owned by Dr Schneider, President of the German Association of Chambers of Commerce. It is housed in Düsseldorf, in a charming eighteenth-century hunting-lodge, and may be seen by the general public. Nearly three million persons a year visit the art galleries of Bavaria alone.

But if visits to museums and art galleries are already popular, there is still plenty of room for them to become even more so—especially with children. That at least is the view of the relatively unimportant museum and picture gallery in Bonn where, besides the traditional visits of school classes with teachers, the children are encouraged to come alone and paint their own copies of the pictures they like most. The scheme has been such a success that 'we can hardly keep the children away,' the museum authorities have said. They have now started competitions among the children for the best copies of paintings in the gallery. Particularly popular, with children and grown-ups alike, are visiting displays of European and oriental art, for which the Villa Hügel, family mansion of the Krupps at Essen, is often used.

THE PRESS

West Germans are great readers of newspapers. Of these there are some 1,300 daily papers, though many hundreds of these are sub-editions, carrying the same main news and features as their main editions plus a page or so of local news for the small town or country area in which they circulate. There are some 600 main editions, with a total circulation of about twenty-one million copies. Included in these figures are 395 larger newspapers serving either the whole country or the larger towns and areas with a circulation of some thirteen million. About 80 newspapers are published in the evening. Roughly four-fifths of the adult population—about thirty-four million persons—read a daily newspaper.

A feature of the post-war newspaper trade in West Germany has been the development of the national paper—in the sense that it is available throughout the country by about breakfast-time. Although long familiar in Britain, such papers were hardly known in West Germany (where newspapers were traditionally published and circulated regionally) until the rise of the press empire created since the war by Axel Springer of Hamburg. His popular *Bild* newspaper and his serious *Die Welt*, bought from the British, who founded it during the occupation, are printed in eight centres and are thus able to cover the country as British nationals cover Britain. Herr Springer has become a controversial figure in recent years, especially among students, partly because of the size of his empire, the largest of its kind on the continental mainland, and partly because his papers are alleged by his opponents to be 'reactionary'—a criticism difficult to uphold if only because they are so varied.

K

Other widely-read press publications are the illustrated weeklies, of which *Der Stern*, with a circulation of 1,584,000 copies is among the biggest. These papers, whose appeal is mainly family and popular—though in the case of *Der Stern* sometimes with highly controversial political features as well—resemble *Life* and *Look* in America, but have no counterpart in Britain. *Der Spiegel*, which is modelled on the American news magazines like *Time*, is immensely successful in its irreverent, pin-pricking way. It has sometimes been called 'the only true German conscience.' *Die Zeit* is a political, economic and cultural weekly paper of exceptionally high standard while the *Frankfurter Allgemeine Zeitung* and the *Süd-Deutsche Zeitung* are dailies in the same category.

SPORT

Sport grows in importance as the number of working hours in the week is reduced, and millions of people spend a large part of their increased leisure either in watching sporting events—above all football—or in practising some kind of sport. One indication of the interest is that 267 sports magazines sell almost four million copies a year.

Football is the most popular sport, though it is followed closely by gymnastics. This may surprise the British and Americans, in whose countries gymnastics on the parallel bars, the horizontal bar, the vaulting horse, etc., are less common. But then cricket and baseball are quite unknown in Germany. These two main sports, followed by athletics, are cultivated in a very lively club life that penetrates to the smallest villages. Winter sports are also very popular, and since there is invariably ample snow in at least three areas of the country (the Harz, the Black Forest and Bavaria), they can be practised by most of those who wish. Other popular sports are tennis and swimming. Every town possesses at least one swimming pool, either indoors or outdoors, and larger towns have several. The motorist in quite remote country areas is likely to find a swimming pool without difficulty

How They Amuse Themselves

when he needs it on a hot summer day. Riding and handball are two sports of very different kinds in which Germans excel. The international riding tournament at Aachen every year is an event of great sporting and social importance.

Local government authorities pay out some £13.4 million = $37.5 million a year to provide playing fields and other sporting facilities. A lump sum of £4.5 million = $12.5 million is also received from the proceeds of the national lottery, while entrance fees to sporting events amount to about £18 million = $50 million a year. Still more money is provided by both the federal and state authorities, for the construction of sports stadiums, swimming pools, athletic halls, etc. The biggest sports stadiums in the country (Berlin, Stuttgart and Frankfurt) can each accommodate 90,000 spectators. There are also a number of motor-racing tracks, of which the *Nürburg Ring*, near Bonn, is internationally famous.

Sport is compulsory in schools, and two hours a week are given to it in primary schools, three hours in secondary schools. Sport in this case includes physical exercises. The importance of this is shown by the fact that nearly one child out of two starting school in West Germany suffers from some kind of physical infirmity, however slight. This, according to the German Olympic Association, is the result of the 'de-activation of the human body by motorisation.' Other results of the same thing, the Association says, are that 70 per cent of all gainfully-employed persons have to stop work an average of ten years before reaching the retiring age, and that heart and circulation troubles account for 42 per cent of all deaths. That is a higher figure than for any other ailment.

Germany is the classic country of the *Wandervogel* (rambler) and it was there that the *Jugendherberge* (youth hostel) originated—not only for overnight accommodation but for folk-song singing and for romantic talk of a specially Germanic kind. Walking or rambling is still popular, and there are still youth hostels, but in an age when young people all have their motorcycles or indeed their own cars and are very sophisticated, not to say rebellious, the overnight guests tend to be rather older—

those who have had their motor cars and discarded them again on the doctor's advice and have taken once more to the bicycle (a collapsible type which has given the industry a new lease of life), or even their feet, in accordance with the original theory of the *Wandervogel.*

HOLIDAYS

Many of those who might earlier have wandered on foot and spent their nights in youth hostels now travel by car and drag a caravan behind them. The plan is not—as might be supposed—to get away from it all, to peace and quiet and solitude—but to get with it, to get with even more of their kind than in a crowded youth hostel or hotel or anything else. The West German young, and the middle-aged and for that matter not a few of the old, spend their holidays on camping sites that are listed for them in guide books. They crowd cheek by jowl, in their caravans or under their tents, on river banks or by the seashore or wherever else the list says. It is the new holiday technique and it is very successful.

As prosperity began to return after the war, there was first a 'gluttony wave' as people who had for long been only half-fed spent all their money on the food and drink that was again available. Next came a 'clothing wave' and a 'housing wave' and then a 'motor car wave' and a 'travel wave.' This meant that people began going to countries from which they had for so long been cut off. They went first to Italy for their holidays, and then Spain. Then they ventured further afield, to Greece or Egypt or Tunisia or the Canaries. It became a kind of dizzy competition to see who had gone farthest. Travel agencies and charter companies, with their organised tours and their all-in terms, aided and abetted, so that holidays abroad were brought within the reach of almost everyone. A federal law guaranteed at least fifteen working days' holiday (eighteen for those over thirty-five) and many firms gave more. The amount spent by West German tourists abroad weighed very heavily in the balance of payments, offsetting in large part the handsome trade surplus earned by exporters (see also Chapter V). West Germans became ubiquitous on the beaches of southern Europe—so much so that the local inhabitants began making remarks that were a good deal less than friendly. But they continued to take the money. Recently there has been something of a reaction among the Germans as is shown by the story of a group of them who were telling each other where they had been on holiday. 'To Greece' said one, 'to Kenya' said another, and 'to Las Palmas' said the third. None of this provoked any comment, but when a fourth said he had been to the Black Forest he was called 'a snob.'

9

Hints for Visitors

VISITORS ARRIVING at the West German frontier need expect no difficulties over passports or customs controls. Officials are as easy-going and helpful as possible within the limits of the regulations, and these are very liberal. Many a new arrival from abroad has been known to tell, as his first story of experiences in West Germany, that 'they just waved me through; I could have brought in anything I liked.' The fact is that the authorities have long recognised that the gain in terms of public relations that comes from light-handed controls at the frontier far outweighs the trifling loss on smuggled tea or coffee, whisky or cigarettes. They are also aware that, as customs duties fall away both inside and outside the Common Market, there are far fewer commodities that are worth smuggling. Even small-scale smuggling has been made largely unnecessary by the duty-free shops at airports. Once inside the country, visitors are likely to find that foreigners are not only accepted but liked. If it is true of the British that they are cool and reserved, even to their own kind, until they know them, and of the Americans that they give a somewhat undiscriminating welcome to everyone, then the Germans tend to give foreigners a preference even over their own people. This is possibly because, as some of them suggest, they were so long cut off under the Nazis from the outside world, and they feel they must make up for lost time. But for whatever reason they will generally try—often in broken English—to be as helpful as possible to the British or American foreigner, and in whatever language they can to the rest.

The motorist in West Germany will find good and willing service at petrol stations. Windscreens will invariably be cleaned as a matter of course, and oil and tyres checked upon request—all without any expectation of a tip. Even if none is given—and it rarely is—the motorist is likely to be wished '*gute Fahrt*'—'good trip'—as he leaves. The traveller by train is likely to need, on any but a short local journey by slow train, a fast train supplement. The charge for these varies according to the category of the train but the smallest amount is 4s=50c and the highest £1=$2.50. The inexperienced traveller who has failed to provide himself with the right supplement in advance can get one from the train conductor, who will make a small surcharge. Otherwise the lowest category supplement can, in the larger stations, be obtained from an automatic machine as well as from the booking office. The highest charge (for the international TEE trains) can often only be obtained at special counters or—with surcharge—from the conductor. The categories for which supplements are required are *D-Zug* (through train), *F-Zug* (long-distance express train) and TEE.

Hotels range from the simplest country inn to the finest international luxury class. The price range is similar—from £1=$2.50 to ten times that figure, or more for a double room with bath. As well as this basic price, there will be a 15 per cent service charge and, since 1 January 1968, an additional 10 per cent added value tax (*Mehrwertsteuer*), which will sometimes be included in the basic charge and sometimes as a separate item. This tax (since July 1968 11 per cent) may also be added to the service charge, so that the visitor is likely to be left with the feeling that the original price quoted bears little relationship to the final bill. In some states there may also be a separate *Getränkesteuer* (drink tax) and in some a *Sektsteuer* (sparkling wine tax). Heating in winter is often charged extra. The visitor will also be expected to breakfast in his hotel, and indeed in most larger hotels he will be presented on arrival with a card giving him his room number and the information that breakfast is compulsory (*Frühstück obligatorisch*). This refers to the standard breakfast, consisting of several kinds of bread, butter, jam, and coffee with tinned milk. Those who want something more or something different can usually get it in the larger hotels, though if they are not very careful they will be served with, and charged for, the standard breakfast as well.

Hotel beds conform to the general German practice, which is to have as sole covering a *Plumeau*—an eiderdown inside the sheets, which are in the form of a bag. Whatever advantages this may have from the point of view of the chambermaid, who can make such a bed in an instant, it is not always appreciated by the visitor—especially the restless one who, if he kicks it off in the night, will be left with nothing at all. The *Plumeau* is not for tucking-in. But most hotels will on request make up a bed 'English style.' Those who like nothing under their heads but a pillow will not appreciate the wedge-shaped extra head mattress on German beds. But if the lower sheet is pulled back it will be found to be detachable and easily removed. Soap is provided (in very small pieces) only in the very largest hotels.

For some years after the war there were many people in many countries whose feelings were so strong about the crimes committed by Germans during the Nazi period that they refused to visit Germany. The British were perhaps the last to overcome these feelings, but even for them the visit of the Queen in 1965 seems to have been a turning-point. From then on they came in much the same relative numbers as visitors from other countries—until the foreign exchange restrictions imposed limits of another kind. But as these pass the numbers will no doubt rise again, and with good reason, since, except for sun, where it cannot compete with the Mediterranean countries, West Germany can offer as much as most, and more than many. Its great variety of architecture, tradition, culture, speech and gastronomy is one of the compensating advantages of its slow and often tortured development towards unity (see Chapter I). But there are also sea and lake and river and forest in rich profusion, so that the taste of the most exacting visitor can be met. If he likes neither sea nor landscape there are great cities like Berlin and Hamburg, Frankfurt and Munich and others, all with their own style and character. Or there are smaller towns of immense architectural and historic interest, from Lübeck or Lüneburg or Goslar in the north, Soest, Göttingen or Limburg in the middle, to Bamberg, Nuremberg, Rothenburg and Ulm in the south.

If coast and countryside remain the greatest attractions, then the visitor is likely to turn to such places as Travemünde on the Baltic Sea or to the chain of the East Frisian and other islands, on some of which, including Heligoland, no cars are allowed. Still in the north, but inland, Lüneberg Heath is magnificent walking country, especially for those whose mountaineering days are past, for it is flat land. A little to the south there is the classic Harz with medium hill-climbing for those who want it. Then there is the Rhineland which, even though highly commercialised, is still romantic—at least on the stretch between Bonn and Bingen where the vine-covered hillsides rise steeply from each bank and where there is a castle on every peak. But for many the tributaries of the Rhine are more attractive—the Moselle, whose wine is as fine as the finest from the Rhine, and whose banks are steeper, and the Lahn and the Neckar (with Heidelberg on its banks), and the Main which, if followed east from Frankfurt where it joins the Rhine, offers enchanting bends in which old towns and villages are hidden from all but the careful gaze. The valley of the little river Ahr, just south of Bonn, is of quite special charm, and produces much of the red wine of West Germany.

The south means the Black Forest, which spreads with varying characteristics from Baden-Baden to Lake Constance, the gentle land of Baden itself, and the ever-impressive Bavaria, with its lush meadows, its splendid lakes and noble mountains, as well as a considerable stretch of the Danube on which such fine old towns as Passau stand.

There are scattered throughout West Germany a large number of hotels with such special facilities as riding, fishing, tennis and swimming-pools, both indoor and outdoor, and these are separately listed in the Varta guide which is on the same lines as the French Michelin. Varta also gives the location of more than thirty old castles in various parts of the country that are open to the visitor as hotels or restaurants or both. Many of them are of great historic interest.

Then there are more than two hundred spa towns—most of which are easily recognised by the word *Bad* in front of the basic name, such as Bad Pyrmont and Bad Neuenahr. Some offer spa treatment, including medicated waters, that may be taken only under medical supervision, while others provide hot and cold showers and baths, sauna and Turkish baths, massage, etc., for any who care to take them. If the waters are not able to cure specific ailments, many people find them a valuable aid to relaxation after periods of intensive work or nervous strain. But as well as the waters, whether for drinking or bathing or both, the spas are always attractive towns that set out to appeal to the visitor. They usually offer fine public parks and gardens, sports facilities and sometimes gambling casinos. Baden-Baden, where round the turn of the century royalty, aristocracy and the rich generally, from all over Europe, gathered for both 'the cure' and 'the games,' is the best-known, but scores of much smaller spas all have their own charm. Many West Germans take their annual 'cure' as a matter of course.

Germans are much more formal than either the British or the Americans in their social habits. This means, not only that they shake hands when they meet and part every day, but that after knowing each other for years and indeed working beside each other in the same office they will not get beyond the *Herr* . . . as a form of address. First-name terms are, at least by British and American standards, rare, and still more so is the intimate pronoun *Du* (the French *Tu*). Even though these standards are tending to relax in more sophisticated circles—possibly as the result of the many British and Americans living in them or passing through—the visitor would be well advised to be very wary of plunging into first names and should, if he knows some German, avoid the *Du* form altogether unless invited to use it. Among Germans it is reserved for the family and very close friends or after it has been 'offered' by an older to a younger person. Its casual or uninvited use can cause much embarrassment—though here, as always, allowances will be made for the foreigner on the assumption that he cannot be expected to know German customs.

It is customary in sophisticated society for a man to kiss the hand of a lady when he greets her—or more exactly to lift her hand to within six inches or so of his lips—but the foreigner should not feel called upon to follow this practice unless it applies in his own country or unless he has become so immersed in the German scene that it comes naturally. The visitor who is invited to a social occasion in a private house may, if he wishes to follow German custom, take a few flowers for his hostess and give a small tip to the domestic servant who gives him his coat when he leaves.

Forms of address are basically much the same in German as in English—*Herr, Frau, Fräulein* for Mr, Mrs and Miss. But there are some important variations and differences that can be of interest and use to the visitor. For example, very many Germans can lay claim to an academic or professional or other title of some kind of which *Doktor* (as a university qualification) is the most familiar. The possessor of such a title can and should be addressed as *Herr Dr*. The surname can, but need not be, added—a considerable advantage for those who have had the misfortune to forget the name. A member of a federal or state government is addressed as *Herr Minister*, a company director as *Herr Direktor*, a bishop as *Herr Bischof*, a judge as *Herr Richter*, and so on.

There is a slight tendency now to poke fun at the German love of titles, and many of the Herr Dr class will ask for the 'Dr' to be dropped. But titles generally are unlikely ever to disappear altogether as forms of address.

With ladies the way out for those who are bad at names is via the highly polite (and always appreciated) form of address *Gnädige Frau*—a phrase not easily translated, but meaning roughly, 'gracious lady.' All ladies of a certain age, whether married or not, are by custom '*Frau X*' and therefore qualified for the *Gnädige Frau* form of address. Ladies below a certain age who are unmarried may be addressed as *Gnädiges Fräulein*, but this is rather rare.

Germans are inclined to say *Guten Tag*—good day—on all and sundry occasions, such as when first meeting in the morning and on entering a shop, bank or office, and as a preliminary to a telephone conversation. Those who wish to conform will reply in kind—*Guten Tag*—while on leaving most will say *Auf Wiedersehen*—good-bye. *Guten Abend* is the greeting for the later part of the day and *Gute Nacht*—good night—for the final parting. *Guten Nachmittag*—good afternoon, is not much used, but the rather curious form *Mahlzeit*—literally 'mealtime'—is often heard for an hour or more both before and after lunch. On taking a place at a restaurant or other table where others are already sitting, it is customary to say *Gestatten Sie*—allow me. Gentlemen tend to raise their hats to each other as well as to ladies, and a man, for example, enquiring his way, will raise his hat both on addressing a policeman and on leaving him.

Index

Adenauer, Dr Konrad, 40, 42, 44-5
Agriculture, 124, 127-9
Aircraft, 122-3
Air transport, 157
Alsace-Lorraine, 28, 31, 37
Angestellte, 104-6, 109-10
Arbeiter, 104-6, 109-10
Armed forces, 64-6
Autobahn, 152, 155

Banks, 140-1
Barbarossa, Emperor Frederick, 75, 82-4
Bismarck, Otto, Prince von, 33-4, 37-8
Books, 166-8
Bormann, Martin, 64
Brandt, Herr Willy, 44
Bundesbahn, 153-4
Bundesbank, 138-9, 141
Bundesrat, 42, 47
Bundestag, 41-2
Bundestrasse, 155
Bundeswehr, 65

Catholic church, 27, 31, 79, 148
Characteristics:
    national, 25
    physical, 14-16
Charlemagne, Emperor Charles, 28-30, 78, 82
Chemicals, 119-20

Common Market, 52, 69, 88, 128, 135, 174
Constitution, 40
Consumer expenditure, 99-104
Currency, 50-1
Czechoslovakia, invasion of by Russians, 39

Education, 145-51
    primary schools, 147-8
    professional schools, 147
    technical colleges, 149
    universities, 149-50
    vocational schools, 147
Electro-technical industry, 119
Elizabeth II, Queen, 58, 176
Employers' associations, 132-3
Employment and unemployment, 133-4
Engineering and machinery, 120-1
Erhard, Dr, 42, 44-5, 68, 135
Exhibitions, 134-5

Federal government, 41-3
Films, 163-4
Finance, 138-42
Fisheries, 129
Food and drink, 97-9
Foreign trade, 135-8
Forestry, 129
Frederick II (the Great), 32
Frederick William I, King, 32

Index

Frederick William II, King, 33
Frontier Defence Force, 58
Fuel and power, 114-16

Gutenberg, Johannes, 86

Handicrafts, 123-4
Hanseatic League, 82
Health services, 111-12
Heating, 96
History, 27-34, 37
Hitler, Adolf, 19, 26-7, 38-9
Holidays, 172-3
Household equipment, 96
Housing, 94-6

Industry, 113-14
Iron and steel production, 117

Kennedy, President John F., 58, 81
Kiesinger, Dr Kurt, 42, 68

Language, 23-5
Lawyers, 64
League of Tax Collectors, 52
League of Tax Payers, 52
Legal system, 58-62
Leisure, 158-60
Local government, 47-8
Louis XIV, King, 31-2
Ludwig II, King, 37
Luther, Martin, 23-4, 82

Mineral resources, 116-17
Ministries, 48-50
Motor vehicles, production of, 117-18
Müller, 'Gestapo,' 64
Museums and art galleries, 168-9

NATO, 39, 65
Nazi criminals, 62-4

Nazi legacy, 62
Nordhoff, Professor, 118

Oder-Neisse territories, 27, 29, 39
Otto I, Emperor, 30

Palaces, 38
Police, 57-8
Political parties, 43-7
Population, 20-3
Potsdam Agreement, 40
Press, 169-70
Protestantism, 27-31, 82, 148

Racial origins, 19-20
Radio, 164-6
Railways, 152-5
Regions:
  Baden-Württemberg, 75-7
  Bavaria, 67-70
  Berlin, 91-3
  Bremen, 84-5
  Hamburg, 82-4
  Hesse, 80-2
  Lower Saxony, 70, 73-5
  North Rhine-Westphalia, 77-9
  Rhineland-Palatinate, 85-7
  Saarland, 87-8, 91
  Schleswig-Holstein, 79-80
Religion, 27
Research organisations, 146
Roads, 155-6

Saar Treaty, 87
Savings Bonuses Act, 1959, 102
Schneider, Dr Gerhard, 68
Schroeder, Herr, 68
Servants, 97
Seven Years War, 32
Shipbuilding, 121-2
Social Security, 104-6, 109-11
Sport, 170-2

Springer, Axel, 92, 169

Tacitus, 19
Taxation, 51-2, 55-7
Television, 164-6
Theatre and Music, 38, 160-3
Thirty Years War, 30-1
Trade, 129-30
Trade Fairs, 134-5
Trade Unions, 130-2

Transport, 152-7

Verdun, Treaty of, 28
Von Stein, Heinrich, 32-3

Waterways, 156-7
William of Prussia, King, 34, 37
William II, King, 38
Willigris, Archbishop, 86